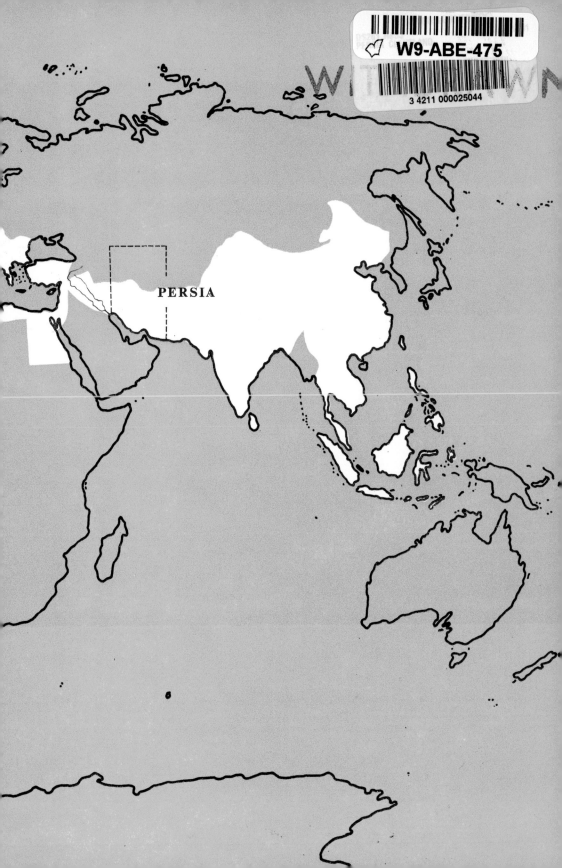

PERSIA

In the same series:

ANATOLIA (2 volumes)

BYZANTIUM

CELTS AND GALLO-ROMANS

CENTRAL AMERICA

CENTRAL ASIA

CHINA

CRETE

EGYPT

THE ETRUSCANS

GREECE (2 volumes)

INDIA

INDOCHINA

INDONESIA

MESOPOTAMIA

MEXICO

PERSIA II

PERU

PREHISTORY

ROME

SIBERIA

SYRIA-PALESTINE (2 volumes)

ARCHAEOLOGIA MVNDI

Series prepared under the direction of Jean Marcadé, Professor of Archaeology at the University of Bordeaux

JEAN-LOUIS HUOT

PERSIA I

From the origins to the Achaemenids

English translation by H.S.B. HARRISON

64 illustrations in colour; 95 illustrations in black-and-white

THE WORLD PUBLISHING COMPANY
CLEVELAND AND NEW YORK

2

5

3

← 1

9

8

11

17

18

23, 24 →

28, 29, 30 →

← 38, 39

43

44

46

METHODS

I

It was not until the end of the 19th century and the beginning of the 20th that adequate resources became available for archaeological work in Iran and increasingly scientific methods for this work were developed. There had, however, been some pioneers. The large trilingual inscription surrounding the bas-relief of Darius at Behistun in Kurdistan (about twenty miles from Kermanshah) was studied as early as 1835, thanks to an English diplomat, H.C. Rawlinson. This ex-officer in the Indian Army was sent as military adviser to Kermanshah, where he combined his political work with oriental studies. In India, he had studied Persian, Arabic, and Hindustani, and when he visited Behistun his interest was immediately aroused by the large bas-relief carved in the rocks on the orders of Darius, who is shown judging conquered rebels. He set to work to decipher the inscription, which is in three languages: Old Persian, Accadian, and Elamite. Rawlinson's expedition at Behistun (1836–1839) can be considered as the first serious study of Iranian archaeology in the broadest sense. Unfortunately war broke out between Great Britain and Afghanistan in 1839: Lord Auckland occupied the area in the course of a military expedition that ended disastrously in a massacre two years later. Rawlinson was obliged to return to India. He subsequently gave up his career there to devote himself to oriental studies, and was sent by the British Museum to Mesopotamia as Inspector-General of English archaeological research. During the years 1851 to 1853, archaeological diggings proliferated in Iran – again this was due to an Englishman, Sir William Kennet Loftus. He knew the region well, as he was a member of the Turco–Persian Frontier Commission and visited South Mesopotamia in that capacity. He was greatly interested in the archaeological sites and spent three weeks at Warka; in 1851, he made some borings on the site of Susa, from which he brought back a large number of figurines.

But scientific field research in Iran did not really start until the French took over the Susa site. In 1884, Marcel Dieulafoy conducted two expeditions there.[4] Aided by his wife, he worked solely on the hill that subsequently became known as the Apadana mound, and brought back "The Frieze of the Archers" and a cornice decorated with kneeling bulls. These two magnificent examples of Achaemenid art are now in the Louvre. This is enough to indicate the importance of the site of Susa (or Shush, the ancient name of the capital of the Persians). Following a mission to Iran in 1889, a French mining engineer, Jacques de Morgan (1857–1924), then Director-General of Egyptian Antiqui-

ties, sought permission for the French to excavate this very promising site. René de Balloy, the French Ambassador to Iran, easily persuaded Shah Nassar ed-Din to agree to a convention granting France a monopoly for archaeological research throughout Persia. The French, financed by an initial grant and an annual subsidy, immediately set to work. "For the first time a French archaeological mission was included in the budget, and it continued to figure in it regularly every year up to 1939. We were subsequently able to organize further missions, but they have never benefited from the same legal, official, and – above all – continuing support."[5] The excavations at Susa were reopened in 1946, and the work is still going on.

Morgan was supported in his investigations by a large team; he obtained the co-operation of a number of scientists, including the Assyriologist V. Scheil, and the archaeologists Jéquier, Gautier, and Lampre; he also employed a young mining engineer, Roland de Mecquenem, who later took over from him. Whatever reservations may be made about the methods employed, the number of finds was impressive. Thus, it is mainly as the result of an agreement signed with the de Morgan mission in 1900 that the Louvre today possesses the finest collection of Susiana pottery. Susa was not the only site explored by the French mission: in 1902, Gautier and Lampre started diggings at Musyan, to the north-west of Susa; another site was opened up at Rayy, near Tehran, in 1909 and yet another (by Pézard) at Bender-Bushir in 1913. These excavations are dealt with in a monumental publication, as yet incomplete but so far stretching to almost forty volumes. The name of this work has been changed several times: starting off as *Mémoires de la Délégation en Perse* (Vols I–XIII), it became *Mémoires de la Mission Archéologique de Susiane* (Vol. XIV), then *Mission Archéologique de Perse* (Vol. XV), *Mémoires de la Mission Archéologique de Perse, Mission en Susiane* (Vols. XVI–XXVIII), and finally *Mémoires de la Mission Archéologique en Iran, Mission de Susiane* (Vols. XXIX–XXXVII).[6]

After the First World War, increasingly systematic excavations proliferated in Iran. They are too numerous to be listed here in full, and we shall merely mention the most important ones, giving the dates. First of all, however, it should be noted that, in 1928, a French architect, André Godard, was invited to Iran by the Government to establish a proper archaeological service, make an inventory of historic monuments, and

have necessary restorations carried out. Between 1928 and 1960, André Godard was responsible for a series of remarkable achievements: the creation of the necessary administrative services, the construction of the Iran Bastan (the Archaeological Museum and University of Tehran), and the restoration of a number of threatened masterpieces, particularly in Isfahan. In 1931, when the market began to be flooded with Luristan bronzes, whose origin was unknown since they did not come from scientific excavations but from clandestine sources, he published a book that is still the standard work on Luristan.[7] This book is all the more interesting in that the findings of the only scientific excavations relating to these bronzes – those of Surkh Dum – were not published until 1938.[8] The year 1931 marked the beginning of completely scientific expeditions in Iran. These were started at Giyan by Roman Ghirshman and Georges Contenau.[9] Georges Contenau, Honorary Curator-in-Chief of the Louvre and author of a handbook on oriental archaeology,[10] died recently. Roman Ghirshman started work with the French mission at Tello in 1930, and the next year he went on to Giyan; in 1933, he began the excavations at Siyalk.[11] Thanks to the work at Giyan and Siyalk, it was possible to establish a relative chronology for the prehistoric levels in the west of Iran.

These two expeditions mark a break with the methods used until then, which had been closer to treasure-hunting than stratigraphic investigation. In 1936, Ghirshman took part in the first archaeological expedition in Afghanistan, under an agreement signed in 1922 whereby France was authorized to carry out excavations there at whatever sites it might choose. In 1941, he became chief of the Archaeological Delegation in Afghanistan. The French, however, were not the only archaeologists working in Iran. In the north of the country, on the southern borders of Turkestan, F. Wulsin, an American, made some soundings at Tureng Tepe;[12] these were enough to indicate the richness of the site, and full-scale excavations were later started. Ernst Herzfeld started work in 1928 on the mound later known as Tell-i-Bakun, some distance from Persepolis; this notable German orientalist, epigraphist, and archaeologist was later put in charge of the American excavations at Persepolis, and died in Switzerland in 1948. The excavations in the plain of Persepolis brought to light a large quantity of splendid painted pottery.[13] In 1931, an American mission explored the site of Hissar, at Damghan, some 220 miles east of Tehran and 45 miles south of the Caspian. The two expeditions of 1931 and 1932 yielded excellent

results. Attention was drawn to this site in 1880 when some painted pottery was discovered there, and it was precisely located by Herzfeld in 1925. This is one of the key sites of the region,[14] and was excavated by E.F. Schmidt. Another, rather similar site was studied at Shah Tepe by a Swedish expedition in 1933. Thanks to the extremely systematic methods employed, it was possible to establish the stratigraphy with only a few borings.[15] Between 1933 and the outbreak of the Second World War, one site after another was opened up: Jamshidi (French expedition, 1933); Chashmah-Ali (American expedition, 1934); Surkh Dum (American expedition, 1934); Choga Zambil (1936); Persepolis (1931–39). After the War, work was resumed on most of the sites; the Susa excavations were taken up again in 1946, as were those at Hasanlu, Azerbaijan, which had been started in 1936. In 1947, the treasure of Ziwiyeh was discovered in northern Kurdistan, while work at Pasargadae began again in 1949. In 1950, soundings were carried out at the Necropolis of Khurvin, 50 miles west of Tehran; this site had been pillaged by peasants who were flooding the market at Tehran with the pottery they had found there. This work, which had been started by an Iranian team, was taken over by a Belgian one in 1954. Round about this time orientalists throughout the world became extremely interested in Iranian protohistory: in 1956, a Japanese team resumed work at Tell-i-Bakun, and in 1957 the excavations at Hasanlu were taken up by an American team. In 1960, a French expedition went to Tureng Tepe, which had not been re-examined since Wulsin had been there; this work is still going on.[16] In 1961, the Iranians were working on the ancient site of Marlik at Rudbar, a small town south-west of the Caspian Sea. The English have started excavations at Geoy Tepe, (1948), Yanik Tepe, (1960), Yarim Tepe (1960), and Pasargadae (1961). All these expeditions are working in co-operation with the Iranian Archaeological Service. And while each investigation may solve certain problems, it usually raises others. Despite the large number of expeditions, the work is in fact only in its early stages and it will be some time yet before any final conclusion can be drawn from it. The first investigations yielding a correct stratigraphy took place some thirty years ago, and thirty years is a short time in which to perfect knowledge in so new a field. It is inevitable that the findings will be to some extent fumbling and tentative for many years to come.

It is obvious that between 1851 and 1965 there has been a radical change in the methods employed. The archaeological techniques used in Iran today have little in common with

those of Loftus. A quick survey of the main developments will give some idea of the ground that has been covered.

In the opening sentence of a book that should be the "Bible" of every archaeologist, Sir Mortimer Wheeler states that "There is no right way of digging, but there are many wrong ways".[17] In fact, methods are constantly changing, if only because there is always some room for improvement. In Iran, progress has been rapid, but only in recent years. The first truly scientific excavations there date back to Giyan in 1931 and above all to the opening-up of Tepe Siyalk in 1933. It is true that archaeologists are always inclined to regard the methods of their predecessors with a certain condescension, but it is undeniable that the excavations carried out in the early years of the present century were devoted primarily to a search for museum pieces that were valued for their artistic qualities alone. A site was considered as interesting only in so far as it was "rich" or "poor" in objects worthy of appearing in a display cabinet. This approach may have served the history of art, but it had little to do with true archaeology.

The principles applied at that time seem completely misguided to us today. The consequences are, in many instances, irreparable: borings were undertaken indiscrimately and abandoned as soon as they seemed unproductive; walls were "followed" to ascertain the plan of a building and were thus divorced irremediably from their archaeological context; fragments "of no interest" were thrown away; in order to date ruins, deposits at the foundation level were eagerly sought, to the exclusion of everything else.[18]

The first large-scale excavations on Iranian soil were those carried out at Susa by the French expedition led by Jacques de Morgan. Today they are considered to have been absolutely disastrous. Attempts have been made to justify them by saying that the methods used were systematic, even modern, and that the only mistake de Morgan made was to publish the results without appending the detailed record of the work that would be essential nowadays.[19] Certainly, the principles laid down by de Morgan would unhesitatingly be accepted by any present-day archaeologist: "Anybody can carry out excavations aimed at bringing curious or commercially valuable objects to light, without bothering to draw any scientific conclusions from them ... But discriminating investigations, aimed at extracting the greatest possible amount of scientific information from

buried objects, demand knowledge and experience, and are often difficult to carry out, since long training and a great deal of method are needed."[20] Unfortunately, when it came to the actual field work, de Morgan acted in a fashion that now seems completely opposed to the true spirit of archaeology. "I thought," he said, "that I was going to find some large building that would at least be in good enough condition for the plan to be studied, which would have involved a special method of working ... But I soon realized that everything was in the greatest disorder and that the significant objects, however large, were sparsely distributed among a great deal of rubble. This realization led me to adopt a working method that might be termed 'industrial'."[21] He defined this method as "systematic exploitation by levels", and for it he employed some 1,200 workers.

"A thousand men are no more difficult to organize than 200. You simply arrange them in squads and group these squads according to the number of major excavation points."[22] A. Parrot has quite rightly compared this type of excavation to road works! Having decided that any stratigraphic work was impossible, de Morgan had only one problem left to solve: that of removing the maximum amount of earth in the minimum time and with the minimum expense. The total height of the Acropolis of Susa is 35 metres (115.5 feet), and this was divided into seven five-metre levels "experience (having shown) that if the workmen threw the earth into the wagons from a height of five metres, the materials would not suffer(!)". All that was needed was to go down regularly from level to level and have the earth carted away as the work progressed. Everything was considered from the standpoint of the amount of earth to be removed. De Morgan justified the procedure as follows: "A general excavation (by the cubic metre) was therefore called for without taking into account the natural levels, which are imperceptible and which it would be childish to try to distinguish."[23] He calculated that by this method, the cost came to 2.25 gold francs per square metre of earth removed. It is quite clear from this that what he was principally concerned with was the "find". The first reports of the Delegation in Persia were thus understandably vague about the links between the objects and the context in which they were found. Yet it is precisely relationships of this kind that form the foundation, the justification, and the aim of all archaeological work – not the discovery of objects worthy of a museum because they are rare, beautiful, or covered with inscriptions. The aim of an archaeological excavation is "explicitly to recover from the

earth objects shedding light on the past of the human race, making full use of everything that may provide them with a context".[24] It has been said time and time again that the archaeological excavation is the only scientific experiment that cannot be repeated. Once it is finished, it is impossible to check the results in the absence of concrete evidence, since the excavator in reaching back into the past is obliged to destroy what he has discovered. The archaeologist thus bears a heavy responsibility. An archaeological site is studied only once, and this basic fact must govern the selection of the method to be used. The application of methods such as those just described has resulted in the irreparable destruction of a number of ancient sites.

In its general aspect, an ancient Iranian site differs little from a Mesopotamian tell or mound. The actual location of these sites in not difficult to trace; whether it is a Mesopotamian tell, an Anatolian "hüyük", or an Iranian "tepe", it looks much the same on the outside: an artificial mound in the form of a truncated cone, fairly high, with a flat top and sloping sides. The dimensions vary. The Iranian tepes are generally imposing: the Acropolis of Susa is 115 feet high, Tureng Tepe more than 100 feet high. The reasons for this are simple: the building material is always the same-crude bricks baked in the sun. These are still used today. Powdered clay was mixed with water and the resulting paste put into wooden moulds. The bricks thus obtained were dried in the sun. Sometimes the paste was mixed with pieces of straw, of which traces remain. This material is eminently vulnerable to climatic conditions: the sun flakes the clay, the rain dissolves it. The buildings in which it was employed had constantly to be restored and strengthened; while they were easy to put up, they quickly fell into ruin. On the four walls a flat roof was placed; this was made of beaten earth on a framework of beams and planks stretching from one wall to the other. Consequently, the rooms were narrow; as the bricks were resistant only when laid in several thicknesses, the walls were often a few yards wide. It was never long before the whole building was laid low by pillage, fire, or simply the effects of rain. Every deposit of ash in a stratigraphic layer indicates the presence of a former "floor" on which the burnt roof of a building has fallen. How was the tepe itself built up? When, for one reason or another, a building was knocked down, it was simplest for the new occupants to heap the remains together to form a terrace and erect the new building on it. Rebuilding took place on the same spot, but at a slightly higher level. Thus the clay bricks of the ancient houses, returning to the dust from which they came,

accumulated one on top of the other and finally formed large artificial hills. And, leaving aside the special conditions prevailing in the Middle East, it should be remembered that every inhabited city tends to gain in altitude. In Paris, for example, Notre-Dame once stood at the top of a flight of steps: today the interior of the building is lower than the square in front of it. The Roman road that crossed Paris from north to south now lies about twenty feet below the level of the present Rue St-Jacques.

Thus, on the site of an Iranian tepe or a Mesopotamian tell, as one set of occupants succeeded another over the years, the presence of each corresponded to a different "layer". The buildings could also be destroyed by natural agencies (rain or wind) when the sites were not occupied; the periods at which they were thus deserted, as well as the periods when they were inhabited, can be ascertained by the archaeologist. A so-called "sterile" layer can be just as important as the others for an understanding of the site. The archaeologist strives to reconstruct the successive periods by minute observation of the sections he cuts across the site and careful scouring of the inhabited areas. Though he may be obliged to destroy in order to advance the work, he will not do so until he has observed and noted everything in the most exhaustive manner. He must even retain material that might, at the present stage, seem useless and unnecessary, for he must never forget that what seems the best procedure today may in ten or twenty years' time be considered as wanton ruination of the site. Again, information that might today appear to lead nowhere may prove of capital importance at a later date. Archaeology is a rapidly developing science, and excavation techniques must accordingly be constanly modified. It would be impossible to anticipate all possible requirements in this domain.

One of the first principles to follow is that of using as few workers as possible. De Morgan employed 1,200 men at Susa, but the work will not be any better whether it is carried out by two men or 300. Obviously, the archaeologist cannot wield the pick himself, he will have to employ others to do it for him. Here careful supervision is essential, and there should accordingly be at least a team leader, four or five archaeological assistants, and one or two architects for recording data on every site. "If excavation is considered as an operation in the surgical sense of the word, the organization of the work must be similar to that of a surgical operation. This implies a pyramid-shaped organizational structure

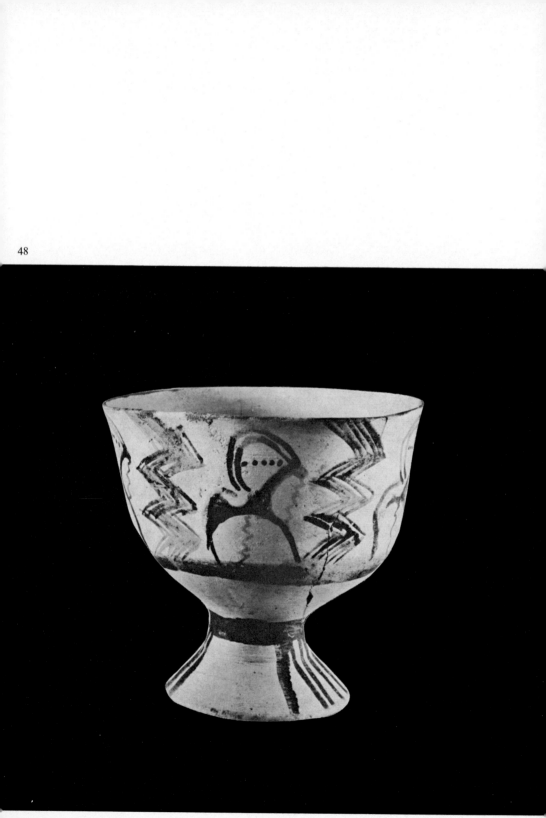

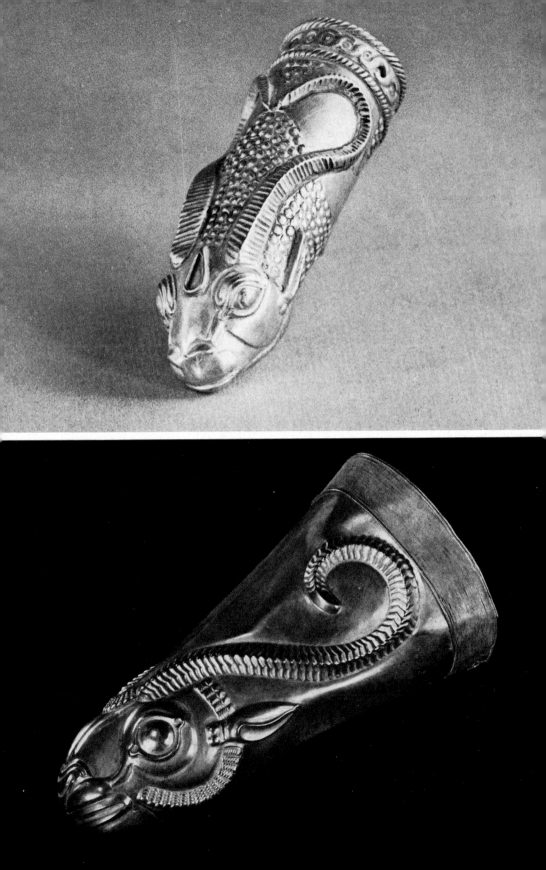

63

of which the incisive point is the surgeon, and not the nurses bustling about in the corridors. Thus, as many experienced excavators are needed as there are excavation points to establish."[25] The inevitable consequence is that a well-conducted excavation is an extremely slow process. All depends on whether the aim is to unearth rare objects or to gain an accurate understanding of the site. No archaeologist has ever been forced to over-excavate; and a limited excavation, carefully carried out, provides much more information that the indiscriminate plunder of a site on a large scale.

Where a site in the Near East has been occupied, the result – as we have seen – is the accumulation in the earth of material of all kinds. The old buildings were simply piled up and terraced, and new ones were built directly on the ruins – hence a succession of different levels, piled more or less regularly on one another, from the most ancient to the most recent. The first duty of the archaeologist is to ensure, with a minimum of doubt, the correct order of these levels, though in the majority of cases he is able to establish only a relative chronology. He must try to restore the stratification of the site, identifying the successive levels that are so many phases in its archaeological "history". To do this, he must carry out soundings, proceeding cautiously at first. As he goes deeper, he can "read" the walls of the excavation and try in this way to follow the order of the different phases of occupation. He must first "delimit" each level as exactly as possible. In theory this is a simple and logical process, but it is much less so in practice. The "reading" of differences in levels is a delicate operation. While they may often be traced by variations in colour or differences in the material they contain, a great deal of experience and flair is needed in order to distinguish them. Truly, as Albright said: "Excavation is at once an art and a science".[26] Again, the stratification is often "thrown out" by the presence of extraneous objects, such as tombs, wells, etc. The interpretation of a wall is accordingly difficult, and it cannot be successfully carried out unless the wall has been suitably smoothed beforehand. "The reading of a section is the reading of a language that can only be learned by demonstration and experience," wrote Wheeler.[27] After having interpreted the various levels recognized in this way, the archaeologist must prepare a clear, precise, and complete account of the walls in the soundings. The excavation thus results in the recognition of a number of successive phases, bearing witness to different cultures. Obviously the archaeologist begins by numbering them from the top downwards. When he reaches virgin soil, he can then abandon this provisional number-ing and call the most ancient culture Level I, the next Level II, etc. Unfortunately, this rational system has not always been applied, and this gives rise to some confusion. Iranian sites such as Giyan have been numbered from the top to the bottom, so that Giyan V is actually the most ancient phase. On the other hand, Siyalk was numbered in a rational fashion, and Siyalk VI is the last period of occupation. Obviously, this rational procedure can be employed only if virgin soil is reached. Otherwise, the last phase recognized by the archaeologist is not perhaps the most ancient, and should not be called Phase I. Thus, the site of Chanhu Daro, in Sind, was numbered from the summit, since a layer of water prevented the discovery of the most ancient levels.

What plan should be adopted for starting soundings? Planning is extremely important, for a badly conceived excavation can very rapidly degenerate into a chaos of trenches and holes that are difficult to supervise. A guiding plan must therefore be established at the outset of operations. It must be possible to record and supervise each excavation. For this, "squaring" is the most rational plan. It should be possible to extend an excavation in any direction, according to necessity or unforeseen developments, without any changes in the initial plan. The most simple procedure is to mark the ground out in squares – not just on paper, but at the actual site, with baulks of earth separating the squares. Thus, at the outset, the excavations will consist of square soundings at regular intervals; the baulks may of course eventually have to come down once the work is well advanced. When this stage is reached, they form an excellent means of verifying the stratigraphy obtained from examinations of the vertical sides of each sounding (known as "sections"). The "squaring" method makes it possible to have a greater number of sections (four per sounding) and thus increases the means of observation and control. It also per-mits new squares to be added in every direction without upsetting the original plan. Each square could measure about 16×16 feet, and should have a pilot trench 18 inches or 3 feet ahead of the rest of the sounding. By giving an advance indication of what the archaeologist is going to encounter, this pilot trench avoids the wastage of archaeo-logical material. Finally, as each square must obviously be used to check the observations made in the others, they should all be dug simultaneously. A special notebook will be devoted to each of them. As for the objects isolated level by level, they should be studied immediately, as far as this is possible. They should all be provisionally recorded and preserved, even if they have to be sorted out later. The great merit of the "squaring" method is that it permits the simultaneous "three-dimensional" control and recording of the levels and materials.

The material that sheds most light on the pre-Achaemenid period is the pottery. Potsherds constitute the most frequently encountered material on any ancient site, and it is therefore not surprising that archaeologists should use them for dating a site at the outset. They enable him to establish a relative chronology based on successive changes in techniques and styles, then to link various levels of different sites on the basis of relationships between the pottery they yield. Such relationships must be established with caution and above all precision, for the dispersion of a certain type of vase over a site did not necessarily occur everywhere at the same time or to the same degree. It must be remembered, however, that no written records dating from before the Achaemenid period have been found in Iran, apart from the proto-Elamite tablets of Susa and level IV of Siyalk.[28] Pottery must accordingly be used as a basis for the classification of Iranian civilizations, at least for the prehistoric and protohistoric periods. The number of scientifically carried out excavations on the Iranian plateau, however, has so far been limited, and any systematic classification is accordingly hypothetical and subject to revision. Be that as it may, pottery remains the touchstone for archaeological deductions.

It must be remembered that, in general, the use of pottery represented an enormous step forward. We know that the terms "paleolithic" and "neolithic" do not merely represent a difference between men who cut stone and men who polished it, but between a civilization of "predators" (hunters and fishermen) and one of "producers" (farmers and stock breeders). The invention of agriculture is undoubtedly the principal turning-point in the history of man. From being a creature dependent on nature, he became one who cooperated with it, producing the necessities of life himself. Agriculture of a very simple kind was already found in the Near East as early as 7000 B.C. Wheat and barley were found in a wild state in western Asia, and their cultivation developed at about the same time as the domestication of animals. The preparation and storage of a cereal-based diet raised problems; recipients were needed that would resist the fire on the hearth and hold liquids. Hence the importance of pottery, which was everywhere a feature of neolithic peasant communities. Gordon Childe has suggested that pottery "perhaps owes its origin to the accidental baking of a woven basket plastered with clay to render it watertight".[29] Certainly, many of the period I patterns at Siyalk, consisting of superimposed lines cutting one another at right-angles, seem to have been borrowed directly from basket-making; but what was at first a utilitarian object quickly became a work of art. A great deal of technical ability is needed in order to make a vase: first of all, a lump of wet clay must be moulded into the desired shape, but if it is too wet it breaks up, and if it is too dry it crumbles. Fired at a temperature of more than 600° C, clay loses its malleability and becomes solid; in this way, the shape of the utensil can be preserved. Fired clay changes in colour, but this can be controlled by changing the method of firing. Thus, when a vase is fired in contact with the air, it will be covered with a reddish glaze produced by the oxidation of its iron content. It can also be decorated with painted or chiselled designs. Pottery, the shaping of clay to the craftsman's will, is the finest manifestation of man's creative power. Sir Herbert Read has stressed this point:[30] "Pottery is at once the simplest and the most difficult of all arts. It is the simplest because it is the most elemental; it is the most difficult because it is the most abstract... Sculpture, to which it is the most nearly related, had from the first a imitative intention, and is perhaps to that extent less free for the expression of the will to form than pottery; pottery is plastic art in its most abstract essence." True, the first potters simply imitated wickerwork recipients, decorating their products in a way that accentuated the resemblance. But they very soon freed themselves from slavish imitation and went on to create works that were masterpieces in their own right.[31] From the aesthetic point of view, the painted pottery is one of the most attractive features of Iranian archaeology. The appropriate classification by series of the pottery found is one of the principal aims of a correctly conceived excavation, and for this reason the methods employed must be constantly refined. These methods are the fruit of a conception of archaeology that centres on the excavation itself as the privileged moment, the key experience. Excavation, it has been said, is not "merely an incidental feature of the chain leading to the study of evidence from the past, a rather tiring way of obtaining objects for scientific scrutiny".[32] It is the archaeologist's most important activity. Whether the subsequent work of historical synthesis will be vague or precise, valid or useless, depends on the care with which it is carried out.

RESULTS

II

Archaic painted pottery

The Iranian plateau has certainly been inhabited since the fifth millennium. One of the most ancient human settlements was identified as such by Ghirshman at Siyalk near Kashan in western Iran.[33] Here an oasis grew up round a spring. The accumulation of dwellings formed two adjacent tepes (north and south). The oldest settlement, Siyalk I.1 at the base of the artificial mound on the north (1,030 × 360 feet, average height 20 feet) did not yield any architectural remains. The earliest settlement must have consisted of rudimentary dwellings made of reeds or branches covered with mud. Starting with level I,2, there were four successive levels (up to I,5) in which fragments of clay walls were found. The floors of the dwellings at these levels were of beaten earth, and there was no sub-foundation to the unplastered walls. The inhabitants of Siyalk I may have practised some form of agriculture and stock-breeding, since a few teeth of cattle and sheep were found there, together with sickles made of animal's ribs combined with flint.[34] The handles of these were carved. The most interesting represents a human figure in a loincloth, standing in a slightly bent attitude – one of the oldest representations of Near Eastern man. Hunting must have been an important activity, to judge from the many sling stones recovered. These are in unbaked clay, extremely resistant, just as effective as if they were made of real stone and much easier to manufacture. The large number of spindle-shaped objects in baked or unbaked clay suggest that textiles may have been produced.

Leaving aside some rather crude dark specimens, the pottery of Siyalk I is red, fairly delicate in conception, and sometimes sprinkled with dark spots caused by faulty baking (mottled ware), or buff-coloured and incorporating chopped straw, which was used to prevent the pottery from shattering during the firing. This type is frequently decorated with black painted designs strongly reminiscent of basketwork. This phase of abstract decoration, dating back to about 5000 B.C., was until recently thought to mark the beginning of painted pottery in Iran. The most frequent designs are black lozenges painted on the inside of the vessel, or zigzag lines. All these vessels were made entirely by hand, as the potter's wheel did not yet exist. The forms were extremely simple: large goblets or bowls with narrow bases, extremely unstable for the most part – they were probably placed in special holes in the floor. At Period I,4, supports in the shape of egg-cups

81

start to appear. Tools were in stone, though copper began to creep in towards the end of the period. At level I,3 a hammer-wrought awl was found, and a pin and a needle were recovered from level I,4. All these objects were hammered, not forged. Ornaments start to appear at level I,4: fragments of bracelets, pearls and shell necklaces. The so-called "cosmetic boxes" – small mortars in stone or terracotta – were probably used for grinding cosmetics with the aid of terracotta pestles.

Tombs were found at every level, the dead being buried under the floors of the houses, or between the houses. All the skeletons bore traces of red ochre: the corpses may have been painted red or – which is more likely – it may have been the custom to sprinkle them with powdered iron oxide at the moment of burial. The absence of figurines and amulets does not imply any lack of religious belief. In fact, the dead were buried in ritual fashion, lying sideways on the ground in a contracted position. One tomb (T.5) contained a polished stone axe within reach of the corpse's hand, and two sheep jaws facing its head. The first period of Siyalk thus yielded painted pottery and evidence of the use of metal and the raising of domestic animals. This period can undoubtedly be linked with the period of Hassuna (Ib) in Mesopotamia, where two types of pottery, one plain and one painted, were also found.

Siyalk II represents an advanced phase of the earlier period. The material found in the 23 feet of rubble at this site gives evidence of definite progress, but shows no real break with what went before. The period represented by Siyalk II (which is also known as the Chashmah-Ali period, after a mound near Rayy that testifies to the same culture) nevertheless brought certain important innovations: puddled clay (pisé) gave way to crude bricks – lumps of earth fashioned by hand and dried in the sun, with fingerprints on one side. The material was first used for foundations and for the floors or rooms. Then, from the time of Siyalk II,2, the walls were built wholly of bricks. Brick walls were more regular than puddled clay ones and less liable to crack. Subsequently these walls were daubed with clay and painted red. The dead were always buried under the mud floors of the rooms. From this period date the first definite traces of the existence of "trade": Siyalk II,3 contained several fragments of Pterocera-type shells, which came from the shores of the Persian Gulf, some 800 miles away. Men were no longer living in isolated groups. Metal was still a rarity. Small copper objects were more numerous, but they were still shaped by hammering. The forms remained very simple (awls, pin heads, bracelets). The use of metal was still at the experimental stage, though metal tools were gradually replacing those made of bone.

The pottery of Siyalk II marks a distinct advance over that of period I. It shows greater refinement; the utensils are smaller, the sides are thinner, and less chopped straw has been added to the clay. This pottery is brick red in colour, with black decorations. The pottery of the last layer of period II was probably baked in a real oven. Thereafter the inner sides of the bowls were fully decorated. Geometrical designs still predominated, but highly stylized animal pictures began to make their appearance. On ceramic potsherds of this period the ibex is shown simply by two short concave lines – for the head and horns – attached to the animal's body which is symbolized by two facing semi-circles connected by vertical lines, "an example of the transformation of a geometrical design into an organic design"[35] showing an amazing skill at stylization combined with a certain vigorous realism. This phase in the Siyalk civilization may be compared with the first settlements of Anau, in the oasis of Merv (Anau I,A), the only tepe in Russian Turkmenistan on which information has been made available.[36] Period V A and B at Tepe Giyan has also yielded a painted monochrome pottery whose decoration is not wholly geometrical. The mound north of Tepe Siyalk was subsequently abandoned and a new village grew up some yards farther south. The southern hill, where Siyalk civilization continued to develop from then on, is larger than the northern one (250 × 180 yards), and also higher (46 feet). The Siyalk III period has been subdivided into seven levels, all of which have been studied on the south hill. It probably covers the greater part of the 4th millennium B.C.

The first period of settlement (Siyalk III,1) was simply a continuation of the preceding period, Siyalk II. It is comparable with an almost identical civilization – that of the first levels of Tepe Hissar (Hissar I,A).[37] In the early days (Siyalk III, 1 to 3), pottery continued to be fashioned by hand. But in the later periods it was baked in a kiln built for the purpose; this was made of clay and rather small. Three openings in the front let the air into a system of circular ducts, which were connected to the oven by eighteen flues; this arrangement made it possible to regulate temperature and draft. At Siyalk III, levels 1 to 3, the pottery was decorated in a greater variety of ways than before, and metal occurred more frequently. But level III, 4 bears witness to a great step forward. There was no break in continuity, however: the forms of the pottery remained unchanged, and the dead – although no longer painted red – were still buried in the same places, in a contracted position. But, from the time of Siyalk III, 4 – or even Hissar I B – copper began to be melted and cast in moulds. Level 4 yielded large pins – more than $7\frac{1}{2}$ inches long – with conical heads, and also the first adze with a bordered hole. At the later levels the amount of material increased: gimlets, pins, flat axes, daggers with a central rib. It is evident that from this period on there were professional craftsmen at Siyalk and Hissar. Pottery, too, became a specialized craft, and the turntable (a simple wooden board placed on the ground, permitting the vessel to be turned during manufacture) came into use at Siyalk III,3. At level III, 4 it appears to have developed into a proper potter's wheel. This was a vital technical development, since it permitted much greater regularity of form and more rapid production. The forms became more daring: a typical one was the chalice on a raised stem, as found, for example, at Tepe Hissar. The clay became increasingly compact and the chopped straw disappeared. The surface of the vase became buff-coloured, and sometimes greenish, as at levels Siyalk III, 6 and 7; in this it resembled the pottery of south-eastern Iran. The decoration remained black but became more complex: geometrical designs, friezes of wild animals, birds, and snakes. The leopard, and especially the ibex, occured most frequently, at first disposed in metopes, then arranged in lines. The saluki – a motif that was to be extremely popular – appeared for the first time. Features characteristic of the style of Susa A (e.g., a reduction in size of the body of the ibex which was increasingly dominated by disproportionate horns) emerged. And more and more often we find Man himself, a slender silhouette, broad-shouldered, the head shown in profile in a stylized manner. During period III of Siyalk, the seal came into use. Engraved stones imprinted the mark of ownership or certified the contents on the clay stoppers of receptacles. The oldest seal was found in III, 1, but this may be an accidental intrusion, for none were found in III, 2 and 3. The excavation report does not solve the problem. But in III, 4 the button-shaped seal with a regular geometrical design appeared. There were also flat discs with a hole in the middle, which were probably worn as amulets.

Thus, phase III of the Siyalk civilization witnessed the introduction of metal-working, the seal, and perhaps the potter's wheel. These constitute a series of revolutionary techni-

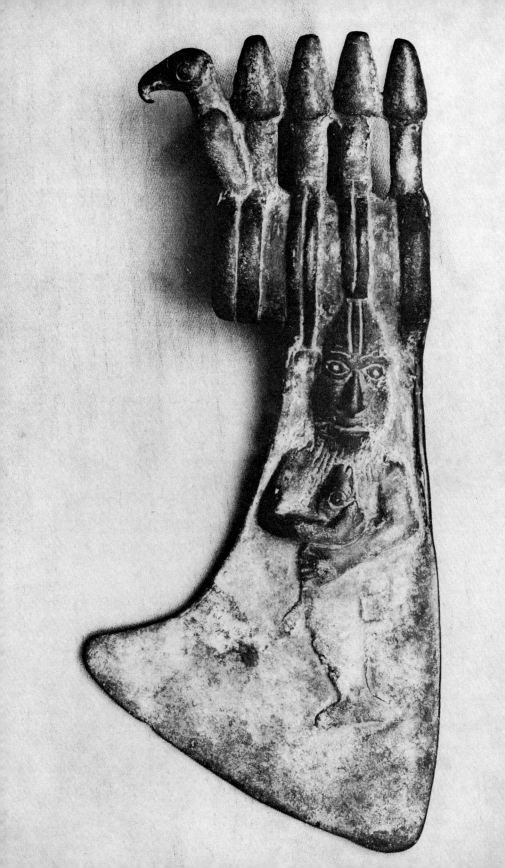

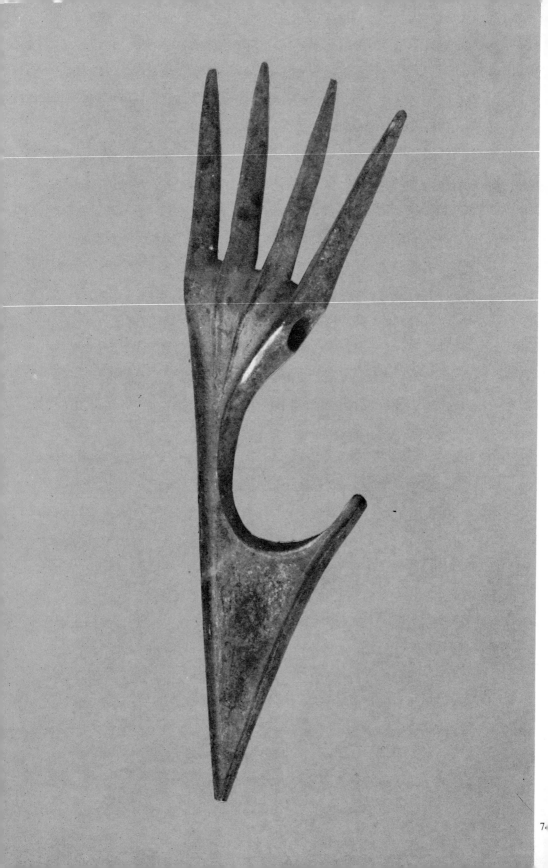

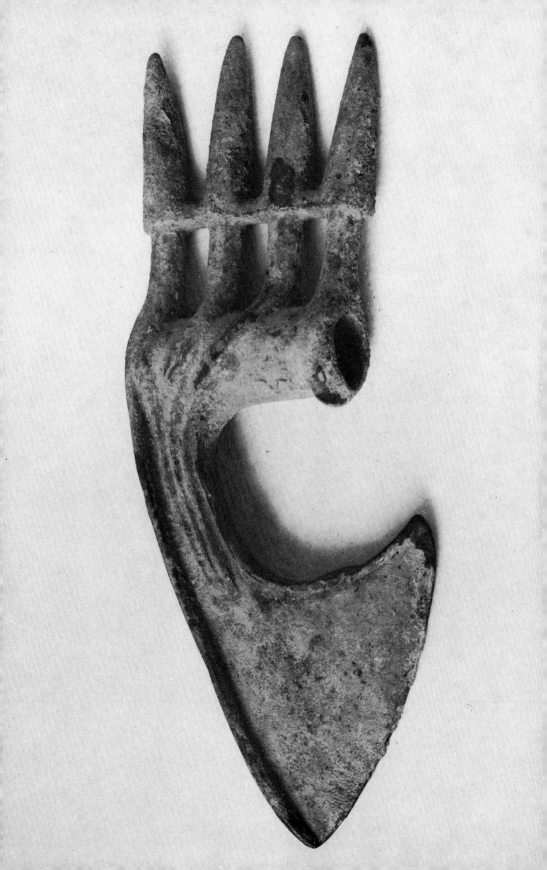

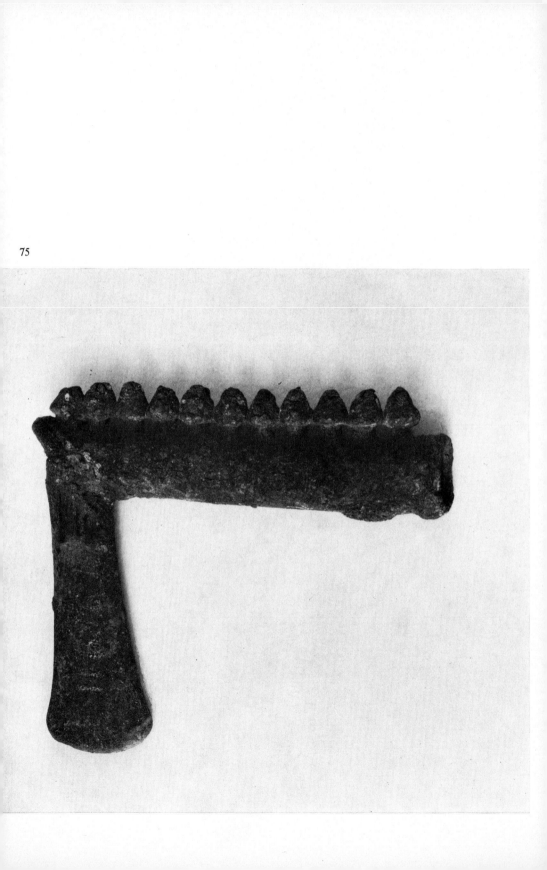

78, 79, 80, 81, 82 →

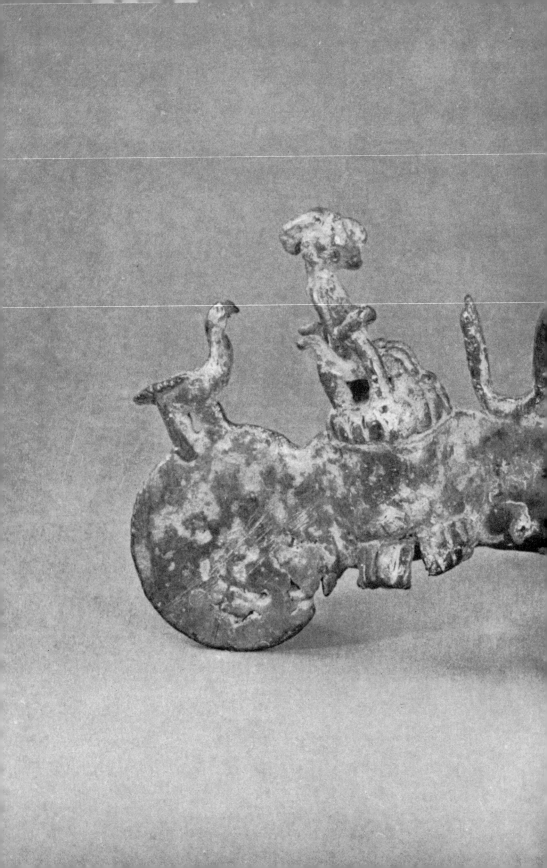

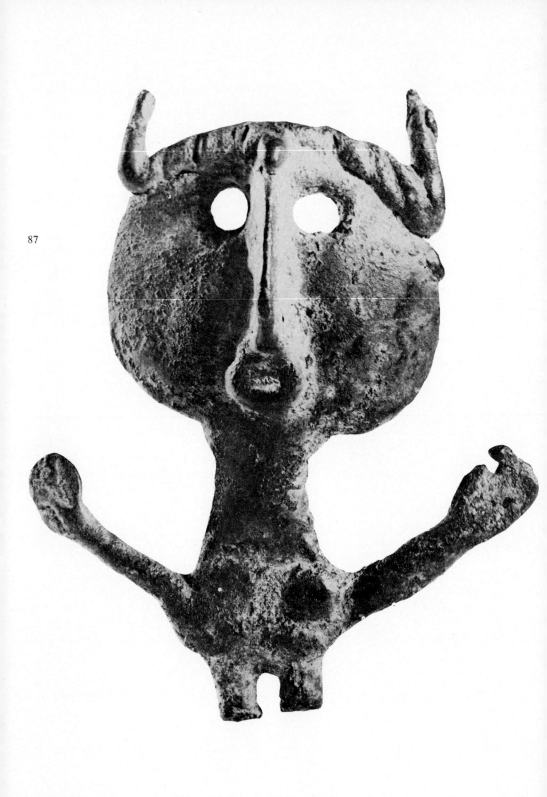

cal advances. Were they invented in the Iranian mountains, spreading later to Mesopotamia? It is difficult to decide. In the present state of knowledge we can only point to certain parallels: phases III, 1–5 seem to correspond to the Tell Halaf and Ubaid periods in the Mesopotamian plain; Siyalk III, 1 and 2 is clearly related to ancient Halaf (where stippled leopard friezes have been found); human silhouettes like those at Siyalk III,5 are also found at Tell Halaf. The geometrical decorations used at Siyalk III, 5 are more or less the same as those of the Ubaid period. D.E. McCown thinks that this shows the Ubaid civilization to be of Iranian origin.[38] But the evidence that might be brought in support of this theory does not take Ubaid I, the oldest phase, into account. Phases 6 and 7 of Siyalk III seem contemporary with the Uruk period. From Siyalk III, 6 we have two vases without decoration and with long spouts inserted obliquely,[39] both characteristic features of the Uruk VII phase. The spout was extremely rare during the whole of period III. This suggests a western influence, albeit a weak one.

The splendid pottery found during the excavations of the de Morgan mission at Susa is undoubtedly of the Ubaid period. Unfortunately this marvellous series cannot be placed in any context. It does, however, show that south-west Iran was one of the first centres of painted pottery. Today this south-western family of Iranian pottery is well known, thanks partly to the French excavations at Susa, and partly to the finds from Susiana (Tepe Musyan, Tepe Ali-Abad, Khazineh, then Jaffarabad, Bandibal, Jowi and Buhallan) and the excavations at Tell-i-Bakun. In 1928 Herzfeld began to excavate near Persepolis, on a small mound that had as yet no name. He continued this work until 1931, in co-operation with Langsdorff, on behalf of the Oriental Institute of the University of Chicago. They called the site Tell-i-Bakun.[40] The four levels of Bakun A yielded richly decorated pottery which seems to prove that the standard of civilization was as high as that at Susa. Numerous conical bowls were found: one of them is decorated on the outside with two wild sheep whose spiralling horns – disproportionately enlarged – cover almost the whole surface of the vessel. Sometimes the animal's body was omitted and only the horns were painted so that they were reduced to mere decorative motifs. These were used in conjunction with purely geometrical designs (checked rectangles, Maltese squares). All these splendid vases were made by hand, but baked in special ovens. Buttons engraved with crosses and complicated designs were used as seals. The style of the latter – like the pottery – justifies the comparison between Bakun A and Susa A.

It was at Susa that the masterpieces of Iranian archaic painted pottery were found. The site of Susa is an imposing mound with three peaks crowned by the citadel, the Apadana, and the royal town of the Achaemenid kings. Since 1897, the French mission has collected thousands of examples of prehistoric pottery there. In the absence of stratigraphy, a classical archaeologist, E. Pottier, distinguished two separate series, Susa I and Susa II.[41] Subsequently four phases preceding Susa I were recognized (Susa a, b, c, and d, from the sites of Jowi, Jaffarabad, Bandibal, and Buhallan), and the former style I was renamed Susa A. Then came three further periods, Susa B, C, and D, with Susa D corresponding to the earlier Susa II and contemporary with the so-called Early Dynastic period of Mesopotamia.

The oldest settlement, Susa A, is known chiefly for its cemetery, which probably contained more than 2000 tombs[42]. This necropolis yielded the pottery that has given Susa A its reputation as one of the most interesting archaeological sites in the Near East from the artistic point of view. The bulk of this pottery is of extremely delicate material, light in colour with a faint greenish tinge. The decoration is still monochrome (black or reddish-brown). The predominant forms are a wide, open bowl, a tall goblet, and a keeled pot with handles. Generally speaking, the decoration is notable for its unfailing sense of composition and its extremely clear and forceful drawing. Every item achieves the perfection, sureness, and balance of a masterpiece.

The most famous example is undoubtedly a large goblet whose decoration is divided into three sections. The principal design, in the lower section, consists of an ibex enclosed in a trapezium which emphasizes the shape of the vase as it tapers towards the bottom. Two curving triangles are fitted together to make up the body, which is indicated simply by the addition of the beard and the tail. The animal is shown in pure profile, with two legs. The curve of the back is continued directly by the horns which are tremendously enlarged and boldly stressed. The perfect curve of the horns, the balance between them and the body of the animal, the stylized simplicity of the latter – all these suggest the end-product of a long evolution. The horns enclose a mysterious design: a series of herring-bone patterns in the centre, with a network of squares on each side, the whole enclosed in a circle. Is this a mere abstract decoration or "a symbolic representation of a plant in a field"?[43] The middle section shows a frieze of salukis with disproportionately elongated bodies which serve to emphasize the rounded shape of the vase. The upper section has a frieze of highly stylized birds whose necks stretch to the rim of the vase. It adds lightness to the upper part of the vessel, while the base is heavily emphasized by a wide, dark band. The whole serves to demonstrate how the painters of Susa combined the figurative with the abstract. "While the salukis are shown as they are, the ibex is used in order to create an effective composition. The birds, with their interminable necks, are barely recognizable."[44] No less characteristic of Susa A are the wide bowls decorated on the inside. Here the artists always made skilful use of patterns that emphasized the rounded shape of the utensil. Here, too, stylized animals appear side by side with purely geometrical designs – that is, if the mysterious designs at present known as *"animaux-peignes"* really represent animals. This period witnessed the appearance of engraved stones used as seals. The designs are almost always linear or employ hatching. The meaning of most of them still remains obscure, though many of them appear to represent protective spirits.

Parallel with Mesopotamia, Susa underwent an urban revolution. Round the year 3000 B.C. there were a number of changes: the cylinder replaced the seal and modelling in the round became more widespread – as is shown by a lion-demon of the Susa C era, a small meerschaum object that gives a remarkable impression of strength (now in the Brooklyn Museum).[45] From Susa, too, comes a terracotta ram (Louvre) which conveys the basic character – the peaceful strength – of the animal so completely that the details are unimportant. There is an amazing wealth of small moulded objects, mostly of alabaster: birds, ducks, bears, toads, small human figures, etc. The end of the Susa C era witnessed an abrupt change in pottery with the appearance of the Susa D style (formerly known as Susa II).

At the beginning of the 3rd millennium B.C. (roughly corresponding to the Early Dynastic period in Mesopotamia) painted pottery reappeared – mainly polychrome, though sometimes monochrome, with black designs on a red background. The best example of this is the series of large polychrome jars decorated with a combination of geometrical designs and realistic figures. A similar kind of pottery was found at level IV of Giyan – large jars decorated with birds.

To the north-east, towards the Caspian Sea, painted pottery becomes increasingly rare. At Tepe Hissar (Hissar II), at the beginning of the 3rd millennium B.C., it gives way to a plain grey-black pottery. This grey pottery was the only kind found at the next level (Hissar III), and it has been found at other sites (e.g., Shah Tepe II) at levels corresponding to the same period. It has also been observed recently at Tureng Tepe where the specimens found had been polished to a high gloss.[46] The problem raised by its appearance has not yet been solved.

Elamite art

Towards 1600 B.C., the Kassites – a mountain people from the Zagros – poured across the Mesopotamian plain and settled at Babylon. They remained there for some six hundred years, splendidly carrying on the Mesopotamian tradition. They looked after the captured towns and built imposing monuments, e.g., the ziggurat at Aqarquf. As the Kassite dynasties had done at Babylon, an Elamite dynasty established itself at Susa in the second half of the second millennium. In fact, it was Elam that finally overthrew the Kassites. It was ruled by remarkable sovereigns, e.g., Untash-Huban, Shutruk-Nahhunte and Shilhak-Inshushinak. At the beginning of the 12th century B.C. Elam reached the height of its glory, under Shutruk-Nahhunte, who invaded Babylonia and conquered the last Kassite. The Elamite armies subsequently advanced as far as Assur. The whole western part of Iran seems to have benefited from the unity thus achieved. At the end of the 2nd millennium B.C., however, a swift decline set in. Nebuchadnezzar I captured Susa, and Elam again "disappeared from history".[47]

The excavations at Susa and Choga-Zambil brought to light important evidence, ranging from great architecture (a ziggurat) to engraved gems, and including bas-reliefs and large and small statues. Little is known of the domestic history of Elam, but engraved gems have enabled us to classify Elamite works of art into early, middle, and late styles.

The early period (first half of the second millennium B.C.) has left no architectural remains, but the middle period of Elamite art – from about 1500 to 1000 B.C. – produced a monument that alone would make it outstanding: the ziggurat of Choga-Zambil in the Susa region. This storeyed tower – an imposing mountain of bricks dominating the desert – is still standing. Of the twenty or so ziggurats known in Mesopotamia (at Babylon, the Etemenanki, at Borsippa, at Aqarquf, Ur, Assur, etc.) none is so well preserved or so impressive in its dimensions (82 feet high) as that of Choga-Zambil. It was spotted during an aerial reconnaissance survey carried out by the Anglo-Iranian Oil Company. The Susa mission was informed and sent a series of expeditions there between 1936 and 1939.[48] Between 1951 and 1962 the site was further excavated under Ghirshman's direction, but the final results have not yet been published.[49]

Besides the ziggurat itself, the excavations have revealed a group of palaces and, in the sacred enclosure, eleven temples arranged in groups of three and four. One of them was dedicated to Inshushinak, the god of Susa, others to Huban, Kiririsha and Ishmekarab.[50] These buildings are enclosed by an ellipsoidal wall (1300 × 875 yards) which follows the line of the hills. Within it is a smaller rectangular wall (330 × 440 yards). The ziggurat itself was dedicated to Inshushinak, the guardian god of Susa. Inscriptions on bricks show that it was built by the Elamite king Untash-Huban. The tower is in the form of a square with each side measuring 112 yards, and three of the original five storeys have been preserved. The building seems to have been put up in two stages. The first comprises the lowest storey only, built as a large open square with walls 26 feet wide except to the north-east where the wall is 14 feet wider. Within the thickness of the walls are vaulted chambers. It is made of unfired bricks. Subsequently the upper storeys were built one inside the other, each resting directly on the ground, with the highest one in the centre. On each side was a monumental door with a staircase leading from it. Three staircases led to the second storey. Only the south-west entrance led to the top of the tower, which probably contained the upper temple of Inshushinak. Beside the ziggurat a palace – undoubtedly a mausoleum – stands above five crypts, probably royal tombs. Built at a depth of 20 feet, they were carefully vaulted with fired bricks bound with bitumen. One of them was never used, two others were pillaged, and two have remained intact. They provide an example of cremation unique in Elam: the bodies there were burnt, together with their weapons and jewels. Perhaps this rite was reserved for the royal family. This group of buildings raises the question of water supply. Fresh water is found only at a depth of 1000 feet. The 1961–1962 expedition, following the line of the outer wall to the west, revealed that the rampart was built on a dyke crossing a large reservoir, which was connected by nine canals to a smaller one. The muddy water flowed first into the large basin and then into the smaller one, becoming clearer in the process. This ziggurat may give us a better understanding of Genesis 11, verses 2 to 4: "And it came to pass, as they journeyed from the east, that they found a plain in the land of Shinar;" – the Shanar of the cuneiform texts, i.e., Babylonia – "and they dwelt there. And they said one to another, Go to, let us make brick, and burn them thoroughly. And they had brick for stone, and slime had they for mortar. And they said, Go to, let us build us a city and a tower, whose top may reach unto heaven." (Authorized Version).

Ghirshman has attempted to reconstruct the place of worship. He thinks there must have been a rostrum bearing the royal thrones opposite the main entrance. In front of the entrance there probably were slabs for sacrifices, shaped like truncated pyramids.

A bronze votive plaque, the Sit Shamshi, found by the de Morgan mission at Susa, shows a ceremony similar to those that must have been held in front of the entrance to the ziggurat. It includes figures in relief and in the round, and measures about 23 by 16 inches.[51] It was discovered in a block of plaster resembling a brick and embedded in a wall. Unfortunately parts of it were damaged during cleaning.[52] The inscription shows that it represents a ceremony at sunrise (Sit-Shamshi) and that it was made at the behest of Shilhak-Inshushinak (1165–1151). This is the only early Asiatic work that "has been preserved in its three dimensions"[53]. In the centre are two small figures facing each other: one is holding out his hands – palms upward – to the other who is washing them with lustral water from a vase. There is a building at each end, one two-storeyed and the other three-storeyed. In front of the higher ziggurat is a sacrificial altar with six small hollows in its top. On either side of the large temple are four small cones, rather like the fourteen slabs set out in two equal rows, in front of the south-east door of the ziggurat of Choga-Zambil (possibly for sacrifices). The altar is framed by two conical posts. Behind one of the figures is a large jar containing the lustral water. Beside it are four stylized trees, badly damaged, a "simplification of the sacred grove that went with the temples".[54] Behind the grove are two basins and a stone post. This unique work, dating from the first half of the 12th century B.C., gives a fairly clear idea of the ceremonies held at Susa at the end of the 2nd millennium. "Never has a liturgical event been shown with greater precision and accuracy. It not only illustrates the Elamite religion, but the whole ritual of the East. The ziggurats recall the Mesopotamian plain, the sacred grove expresses the veneration in which the Semites held every green tree, the large jar recalls Apsû and the 'brazen sea', the two columns would later have a place of honour in the sanctuaries of Tyre and Jerusalem."[55]

Elamite art of the middle period has left a legacy of very fine works in the round. The most noteworthy is the statue of Queen Napir-Asu, the wife of Untash-Huban[56] (c. 1266–1246 B.C.). Unfortunately this bronze statue has been broken (the head and left arm are missing), but it is the largest metal statue (3,860 lbs in weight) that has been found in the Near East. Even in its mutilated state it is more than 4 feet high. A marvel of smelting, considering the poor methods available at the time, it was cast in two parts (as a reinforcement, molten bronze was poured into the interior) and is a perfect piece of work. The queen is shown in an attitude of prayer, with folded hands. She is wearing a ring and a bracelet. Her dress, though very simple, is shown in minutest detail (folds, embroidery, fringe). Her hands are considered the most remarkable feature. They are delicate and tranquil, and contribute greatly to the overall impression of elegance.

Another good example of Elamite metal work is a bronze head of an Elamite, now in the Metropolitan Museum of Art in New York. The face has a quiet, serious, almost severe expression. The hair is held by a sort of turban made of crossed bands. It may be compared with a more recent terracotta of a Susan, with a similar severe, disillusioned expression – a real portrait in clay and not just a stereotyped figure.

From Susa, too, we have two statuettes of worshippers, one in electrum, the other in silver. Each carries a sacrificial offering – probably a kid – under the left arm. The other arm is raised in a gesture of worship. The workmanship of the faces appreciably resembles that of the bronze head of the Elamite. These two figures date from the 13th–12th century B.C.[57] Also noteworthy, in a very different field, are the bas-reliefs carved in rock – a tradition that was continued in later periods. The most interesting are at Malamir, in the Qul-i-Fir'un ravine. The figures are always executed in flat relief, rather stiffly, and are often tall and dressed in long robes coming to below the knee. They are almost invariably shown in stiff, awkward lines – the prototypes of the Achaemenid processions.

The Luristan bronzes

During the nineteen-thirties the clandestine market in oriental antiques was flooded by a large quantity of bronze objects which were said to have come from the mountains – or rather the high valleys – of Luristan. In the autumn of 1928, a Luristan peasant discovered a tomb while ploughing. The vault contained metal objects, which he straightway sold at Harsin, the nearest town, some 25 miles from Kermanshah. Antique dealers immediately hurried to Harsin and bought up everything that the peasants brought them. Thus, for a time the bronzes were known as "Harsin bronzes". Since then, numerous museums and private collectors[58] have assembled large series of them. For a long time the region was too unsafe for any scientific expedition to be sent there, and this encouraged clandestine excavators. The only site that could be investigated successfully was the sanctuary of Surkh Dum.[59] Apart from the material found there, all the bronzes came from unsupervised excavations. This accounts for the initial uncertainty concerning their chronology – the dates suggested ranged from the beginning of the 2nd millennium B.C. to the Achaemenid period. A. Godard who made the first inventory of these objects in 1931,[60] travelled extensively in the area, which consists of long parallel mountain ranges with large intervening valleys, connected by passes at an altitude of some 10,000 feet. One of these high valleys is described as "a huge labyrinth of hills between two lines of gigantic mountains ... no houses, no trees, but, as far as the eye can see, russet hillsides, some black tents and ... the Kassite necropoles".[61] These burial-places are nearly all alike, and Godard has described one he considers typical, that of Tell-i-Ab, the hill of the water: "A spring flows from a small rectangular basin with stone curbs, widens into a pond dug by the temporary inhabitants of the place to water their animals, then divides into several irrigation canals and, a few hundred yards farther on, disappears into the ground."[62] Beside the spring was a mound, undoubtedly covering the remains of a circular enclosure, with the necropolis at its foot. These burial-places are extremely easy to spot. In this valley where water is so scarce, the settlements – and the burial-places – are always found beside a spring. "The Luristan peasants soon worked out a handy formula for antique-hunting: 'Find a spring, and beside it you will find a necropolis.' It was simple and infallible."[62] The tombs are mostly in the form of

91

92

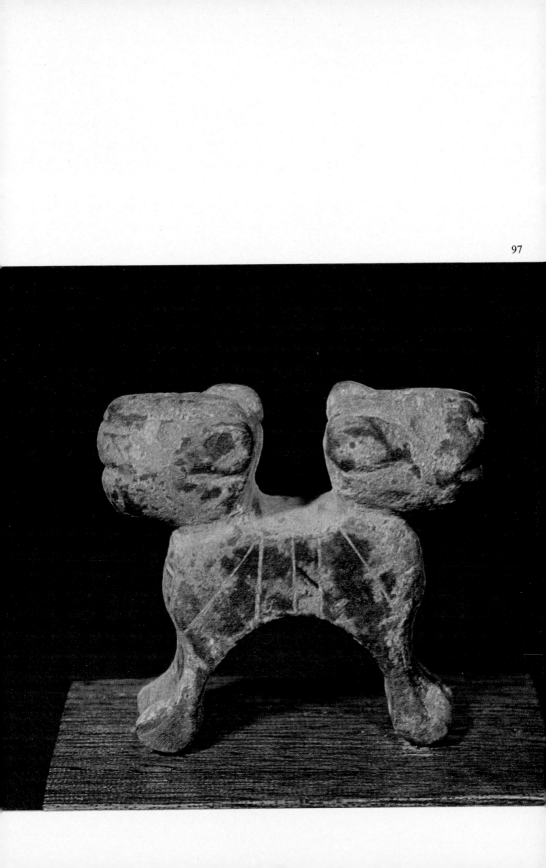

100, 101 →

small stone-lined chambers, usually with four walls and a roof consisting of one or more flagstones.

Luristan has yielded thousands of objects. Here we can only deal with some of the most characteristic. There are large series of weapons: daggers, swords, arrow-heads, lances, axes, etc. We must, however, distinguish between what is peculiar to Luristan and what is not. The dagger most commonly used in Luristan was made of bronze in a single piece; the hilt was grooved and had inlaid wood or bone plates which were held in place by two tabs. It was simply a copy of an earlier, non-Luristan type. The famous digitated axes, on the other hand, were peculiar to Luristan. Most of them had a casing that was open at both ends. Some are very richly decorated – one shows an archer about to shoot an arrow – and a great number of them were ceremonial weapons. The edge is often at right angles to the handle instead of being parallel with it, and sometimes there is an ornament projecting from the upper part of the blade. Judging from the excessive curve of the edge and the useless decorations, these weapons were not used for real fighting but were intended simply for show.

There were many personal ornaments: torques, bracelets, ear-rings, necklaces, and pins. Pins especially were found in large numbers. Some are decorated with animal heads, some with elaborately worked plaques, and some with women's heads set in discs that seem to be derived from those with umbos at the centre. Also noteworthy are the buckles, which seem – like the pins with discs – to be a form of ornament imported from the Caucasus. Important, too, are the pieces of harness, shaft-ends, bits, and rein-stalls. The knights of Luristan were probably buried with their weapons and the harness of their mounts. Plain at first, horse's bits soon became highly decorative, particularly when used as funerary offerings, or rather as head-rests for the dead. The cheeks of the bits were usually shaped like real or imaginary animals. This gave the bronze smith almost unlimited scope: thus we find not only the typical stocky, spirited horses with very small heads, but also hybrid and monstrous animals, griffins, winged sphinxes, etc. There are a great many "idols", usually consisting of an elongated figurine, surrounded by other figures or objects, on a base. The most popular subject is the old Mesopotamian theme of Gilgamesh, treated in a new way. The Sumerian hero, the tamer of animals and conqueror of monsters, has been transformed into a protector of the shepherd's flocks. The idols often have two faces and are shown struggling with monsters: the hero taming wild beasts was a basic Oriental theme and is found again in the Achaemenid period. There are other items that have not yet been satisfactorily identified: were they pieces of harness transformed into ornaments? For lack of a better word, we must call the large decorated rings "pendants". They are like those in the Coiffard collection. "A flat ring with a fastening at the back was surmounted by two man-faced bull's heads framing a wild sheep's head, with vast ringed horns, confronted by two leopards – a masterpiece of imagination and balance as well as of metal-working technique."[63]

From the Pusht-i-Kuh region we have a bronze statuette – the only large item of its kind from Luristan. It is 15 inches high. We can get no help from the inscription – in Neo-Babylonian cuneiform characters – that is carved on the bottom of the skirt. It may date from 600 to 500 B.C., but the effigy itself is older. The place mentioned in the text is unknown. The statuette guards its secret. Is it a local deity carried off as loot? Whatever the answer, it is the first known example in Luristan of a statuette in the round. Godard has linked the Luristan bronzes with the history of the Kassites, an Asiatic people that occupied the Zagros region at a very early date. In the 16th century B.C. these mountain people overran the Mesopotamian plain and founded a dynasty at Babylon. Their domination lasted for several centuries, but in 1160 they were driven back by Shutruk-Nahhunte, the king of Elam. Godard thinks that this episode in Kassite history can be used to date the Luristan bronzes. If, in fact, their production coincided with the zenith of Kassite power, traces of them would have been found in the subject territories. But, as Godard has noted, ... until now no Luristan bronzes have been discovered in the Mesopotamian plain. Excavations conducted on the site of the Kassite town of Dur-Kurigalzu have not yielded a single one ... How can we explain this total absence of Luristan bronzes ... in the Mesopotamian plain and their abundance in the Zagros mountains? There seems to be only one possible answer to this question. The Luristan bronzes did not yet exist at the time of the Kassite occupation of Babylonia. They appeared later, when the invaders had returned to their mountains."[64]

We must exclude certain bronzes of which very much older examples have been found in Mesopotamia, such as the very characteristic daggers made in a single piece with wood or bone decoration on the hilt.[65] Schaeffer has found some at Ras Shamra and has fixed their dates at between 1450 and 1365 B.C.[66] Daggers of this kind had been brought to Luristan as offerings, e.g., the dagger in the Louvre inscribed with the name of King Marduk-nadin-akhe of Babylon (12th century B.C.). Other objects (axes and picks) were made in Mesopotamia and brought to the mountains by way of trade, or were simply copies. The true Luristan bronzes – which were much more highly decorated and elaborately worked – must have been produced after the Kassites returned to their mountains, i.e., after the 12th century. Luristan art must have achieved its peak towards the beginning of the 1st millennium B.C. It disappeared after the defeat of the Kassites by the Assyrians in the 7th century B.C.

This is Godard's thesis. But Ghirshman whose views are confirmed by the work of such Soviet scholars as Piotrovskiy, Malikishvili, and Diakonov, attributes the art of Luristan to the Cimmerians. "From the early decades of the 8th century B.C. we find Cimmerian mercenaries in Assyria, and others allied to the rebellious Medes. We can therefore conclude that this people had divided into two groups, one of them pushing towards Asia Minor while the other moved towards the east of Assyria to a country that continued to have a Kassite name – Luristan."[67] The Cimmerians were nomads and horse-breeders, and the mountains of Luristan obviously suited them. This opinion clearly disagrees with the attribution of the Luristan bronzes to the Kassites of the 8th and 7th centuries B.C. Other scholars point out the extremely mixed nature of the objects classified as "Luristan". J. Deshayes considers that Luristan was a metal-working region which – at a rather early date – played an important part "in the creation of many forms and their diffusion through Assyria and northern Syria – although this does not mean that it did not continue to be an important metal-working centre until a much later period".[68] He establishes a connection between Luristan art and the Hurrians. He thinks that most of the influences that are usually thought to come from the Hurrians (for instance, the love of exuberant decoration) really come from Luristan. He also maintains that the composite forms of Luristan often go back to the second half of the 3rd millennium B.C. He dates the digitated axes from the second half of the 2nd millennium B.C., between the first dynasty of Babylon and the second dynasty of Susa, although he admits that some types remained current until the beginning of the 1st millennium B.C.

Necropolis B at Siyalk

The excavations at Tepe Siyalk have revealed two necropoles, A and B, 270 yards south of the Tepe.

The first (necropolis A) where some fifteen tombs were brought to light, has yielded a grey-black monochrome pottery, tools, and jewels that enable us to place it chronologically at the end of the Bronze Age. Nothing connects these finds with Siyalk IV, the preceding period of the site. There is a long gap between the two which has never been satisfactorily explained. The connection between the grey-black pottery and the similar, but much older, pottery of Tepe Hissar III C is also rather obscure.

The second necropolis (B) is unrelated to the first. The excavator has stated that "the civilization of necropolis B had no links whatever with that of necropolis A".[69] The manner of burial in necropolis B is clearly different from that in necropolis A, and this usually implies a change in population. Some two hundred tombs have been studied in necropolis B, which is separated from the settlement proper. The cemetery was originally at ground level, but the subsidence of the soil over the centuries had gradually buried the tombs. A pit was dug in the ground and the walls – unlike those of the Luristan tombs, and this fact is important for relative dating – were never lined with stones. The dead were laid to rest with a great many funerary objects and then covered with earth. A mound of earth was finally raised above the pit and covered with large stone slabs, laid in ridges, that made it look like a nordic house with a double-pitched roof.[70] Only 71 of the 218 tombs opened by the Ghirshman mission were found intact. Necropolis B has yielded mainly pottery. For tomb 15, for instance, the excavation team reported: "twenty-seven jugs, bowls, plates and jars, including seven with spouts".[71] From this, the following conclusion was drawn: "It is probable that all this pottery did not belong to the dead man, but that his family and friends, after taking part in the funeral rites which were probably followed by libations and a meal, left their own dishes to be buried with the dead man's. This would explain the presence of some rather small and sometimes chipped vessels side by side with well-preserved ones of indisputable artistic value." Typical of the material found is the large painted jug with a long spout; such vessels were too fragile for daily use and were intended for religious purposes, probably libations. They are clearly imitated from metal objects, and even reproduce features that would be useless in pottery, such as rivets. In shape they resemble birds, and this resemblance is emphasized by the decoration. The spout is often ringed by sharp zigzags reminiscent of feathers; there are often eyes and sometimes a fringe of small triangles that looks like a crest. On the belly are decorative motifs, usually painted in dark red on a light background: stylized animals or purely geometrical designs (chequered patterns, circles with crosses, rosettes). Sometimes both types of motif are used side by side on the same vase. Animals – real or imaginary – occur much more frequently than human figures (which appear on only three vases). The bodies in necropolis B were buried with their weapons and crested helmets, and were dressed in close-fitting coats.

According to the excavator, necropolis B dates from the beginning of the 1st millennium B.C. and is connected with the arrival in Iran of the Iranian tribes who settled on the plateau at that time. In Ghirshman's opinion, the whole of the necropolis dates from between the 10th century B.C. and the end of the 9th or beginning of the 8th.[72] He bases this conclusion partly on a study of the skulls: those in necropolis B differ radically from those preceding them on the site. Indirect confirmation is given by the changes in burial practices. At the southern end, moreover, there is a great terrace, some 3000 square yards in area. The lord's dwelling probably stood on this artificial hill, dominating the lower districts at the foot of the castle. This suggests a completely new type of social structure and the settling of new inhabitants from another region. The town contemporary with necropolis B was destroyed suddenly. From that moment lifeceased on the site, which Assyrian armies probably took by storm in the 8th century B.C.

Hasanlu

The site of Hasanlu is in Azerbaijan, in the Solduz valley, south-west of Lake Urmia. Excavations were started in 1936 and resumed in 1947; from 1957 they have been carried out by an American expedition led by R. Dyson and sponsored by the Philadelphia Museum. The citadel of Hasanlu has been linked with the Mannians whose presence in

Azerbaijan is attested by the Assyrian annals. The Mannians were thought to be the successors of the Hurrians of the 2nd millennium B.C. In their annals the Assyrians referred to the country of "Mannai". The Mannians are also mentioned in Urartian inscriptions dating from the beginning of the 8th century B.C. It was probably at that time that the citadel of Hasanlu was destroyed.[73]

Hasanlu was a small town dominated by a citadel. The latter was surrounded by a fortified wall and used as a refuge by the inhabitants. The houses themselves and the necropolis lay outside the ramparts. The walls were imposing, probably some 30 feet high and 10 feet thick, and the whole was reinforced at intervals by projecting towers. Two buildings of the citadel have so far been cleared – halls with columns, of which only the bases have been preserved. Between these buildings are two smaller structures, the "House of the Pearls" and the "House of the South". A golden bowl and a silver and electrum cup were found near the first two buildings.

The golden bowl of Hasanlu – found beneath the skeleton of a man who was carrying it off – is outstanding for the quality and nature of its decoration. The whole surface is adorned with mythological scenes. On the upper part three deities on chariots, one behind the other, are approaching a priest who holds a goblet. Behind the priest are two servants leading sheep. The three deities are probably the earth, the sun, and the storm god, the only one whose chariot is drawn by a bull, his symbolic animal. Beneath is a mysterious battle scene: a figure holding a tiny shield in each hand is shown confronting a monster, half man, half mountain, the mountain part ending in three dog's heads. This scene is linked with the one above by a stream which issues from the bull's mouth and flows down to the monster. Beside the battle scene is a figure presenting a child to a seated god. Farther on is a Syrian goddess who is casting off her mantle to reveal her naked body. The myth depicted is probably a Hurrian one. It has come down to us in a Hittite version, and this is hardly surprising since the Hurrian and Hittite religions were curiously intermingled. The Hasanlu goblet appears to recount the myth of Kumarbi, father of the gods, who was threatened by Teshub, the storm god. To defend himself, he begot the hero Ullikummi out of a rock. The mother goddesses helped to deliver the child and placed him on the knee of his father, who hoped that he would defeat the storm god. The infant monster grew rapidly, came out of the sea, and forced the storm god to fight him. The latter was defeated at first, but with the aid of Ea, the Sumerian god of fresh water and magic, he was the victor in a second battle.[74] The scenes on the Hasanlu goblet probably depict this Hurrian version of the myth of Cronus. It is tempting to connect this splendid piece with the gold goblets found recently in the Caspian provinces, especially at Marlik,[75] and the undoubtedly more ancient cup of Kalardasht (Mazanderan) found by chance in 1934.[76]

A silver and electrum goblet has also been found at Hasanlu. Several scenes are depicted on it, the most interesting being a victory scene. This shows two figures on a horse-drawn chariot: one is driving the animals, while the other is turning back and shooting at his enemies with his bow. The subject and composition are typically Assyrian. Other objects that have been unearthed include enamelled tiles – one of them showing a bull with a man's head – a knife hilt decorated with gold cloisonné, etc.

The pottery is grey, with red and black variations, and is comparable with that of Khurvin. Its relationship to the earlier grey pottery of northern Iran raises a problem. It seems probable that it was influenced by metal prototypes, and the black kind, which is very thin, has so far been found only in buildings. The grey pottery, on the other hand, was used as a funerary offering. It is thicker and much less elegant. The phases of the Hasanlu pottery have been dated by the Carbon 14 method: the era of grey pottery started about 1250 B.C.[77] When this era ended is much less certain – probably at the beginning of the 8th century B.C.

The Treasure of Ziwiyeh

Over fifteen years ago a group of gold and ivory objects was discovered in northern Kurdistan, near the town of Ziwiyeh.[78] This treasure is said to have been found in a bronze sarcophagus and almost certainly consists of funerary offerings. In the 7th century B.C. this was the land of the Mannians, who at that time were allied with the Medes against the Assyrians. After the fall of Mannai, the Scythians settled there. The treasure of Ziwiyeh probably came from the tomb of a Scythian prince. It is made up of objects in a wide variety of styles – Assyrian, Urartian, Medean, Scythian, etc.

Among the most noteworthy pieces are the Assyrian decorative plaques of gold and ivory. Other ivory plaques – imitations of Assyrian objects dating from the reign of Esarhaddon– were the product of local craftsmen. The most important items are Urartian. In the second half of the 9th century B.C., the kingdom of Urartu grew up round Lake Van and subsequently extended from the south of Lake Urmia to the Black Sea. It was finally annexed by the Medes at the beginning of the 6th century B.C. The plaques and statuettes with inlays and also the breastplates are of Urartian workmanship. While the details of the decoration on the breastplates are almost all Assyrian, the breastplate itself is an Urartian rather than an Assyrian adornment. Typically Urartian, too, are the *protomes* of griffins and lions that probably decorated a cauldron.

The specifically Scythian objects must be considered separately. The best known is a large gold-studded silver dish, decorated with concentric circles of various Scythian motifs; these suggest that it dates from the 7th century B.C. The general composition bears a fairly close resemblance to that of the shields of Toprak Kale.[79] The number of solid gold jewels, bracelets, torques, chains and ear-rings, bear witness to a taste for luxury. The treasure of Ziwiyeh testifies to extensive trade with other areas, and reveals a desire to make a coherent whole of heterogenous parts. This desire was not fulfilled. Referring to the "stamp of Scythian art" which is clearly perceptible in a number of objects that were nevertheless closely linked with other civilizations, Ghirshman suggests the presence of a royal Scythian workshop where local craftsmen based their work on 8th- to 7th-century Oriental iconography without really understanding it and were unable to integrate it harmoniously.[80]

The Achaemenid Period

The Achaemenid dynasty created the largest empire that had yet been known: it eventually embraced Iran, Mesopotamia, Syria, Egypt, Asia Minor and western India. Its

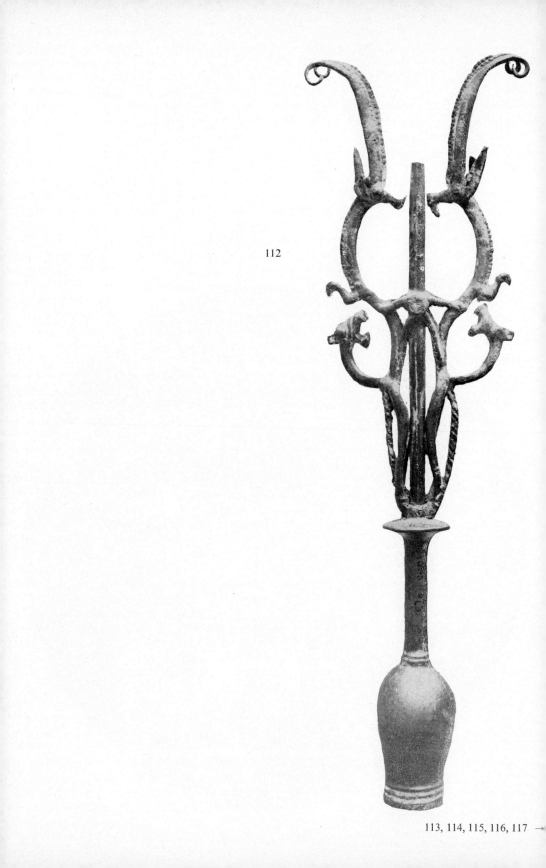

112

113, 114, 115, 116, 117 →

formation was amazingly quick: the period of conquest lasted barely thirty years. More striking even than this rapid expansion was the historical importance of Darius' empire. Built up through a series of quick victories and comprising different lands and peoples with cultures ranging from Asiatic Hellenism to those of Egypt and Mesopotamia, it nevertheless managed to endure. It was able to evolve an administrative system sufficiently flexible to respect the individuality of each people while maintaining the fundamental unity of government necessary to an empire.[81] It also achieved a synthesis of all the art forms it encountered, notably in Assyria, and to an even greater extent in Egypt. The Achaemenid empire lasted for more than two centuries (539–331 B.C.). This is tremendously long when we consider its composite nature, and could only have been achieved by despotism. Thus its art and architecture were wholly based on the glorification and worship of the king – a monarchical art that sought to unite the heterogeneous contributions of the subject countries in one imposing whole.

A brief historical summary

In 559 Cyrus, of the Achaemenid clan, became King of Anshan. He was descended from an eponymous ancestor, Achaimenes, and belonged to one of the ten Persian tribes settled in the south-west of the Iranian plateau, in what is now Fars. At that time the Kingdom of Anshan – more or less linked with Elam – was a vassal state of the Kingdom of the Medes. But between 556 and 549 B.C. Cyrus rebelled. King Astyages of the Medes hastened to the spot to suppress the rebellion, but was defeated and made prisoner. Ecbatana was captured and pillaged. Persia annexed the entire kingdom of the Medes, and Cyrus founded one of the first great Achaemenid capitals, Pasargadae. The year 546 witnessed the famous campaign against Lydia and its king, Croesus, who was defeated and taken prisoner. Lydia became a satrapy and, one after the other, the Greek cities of Asia Minor were subjected. The whole of western Asia Minor was subdued. In 539 Cyrus moved down the Tigris and entered Babylon. Nabonidus was taken prisoner, and the vassals of the Babylonian kingdom came "to kiss the feet" of their new sovereign.

By then the Persians had conquered practically the whole of the Near East. This rapid and easy success has sometimes been attributed to fervour in the cause of Zoroastrianism, although the Achaemenids – far from seeking to spread a new religion, as the Arabs did later – were extremely tolerant and respected the religions they encountered. There are many instances of this – the return of the deported Jews, who were permitted to rebuild the Temple, and the fact that at Babylon Cyrus presented himself as the favourite of Marduk, whose "hands he took", and restored the temples when he entered the city. It is difficult to explain the military superiority of the Persians. They were certainly capable of quick action and were not above trickery and corruption; again, Persian gold worked miracles. About the organization of the empire at that time – which must have been remarkable since there were no disturbances during Cyrus' lifetime – we know practically nothing.

On Cyrus' death his eldest son Cambyses (530–522 B.C.) undertook the conquest of Egypt. The Pharaoh Psammatichus was encircled at Memphis and had to capitulate. In June 525 the kingdom on the Nile was subjected. Cambyses died in 522. After the episode of Gaumata the usurper, a distant relative of Cyrus, a descendant of a younger branch, was chosen as king under the name of Darius I (522–486 B.C.). The age of conquests was past, and the time had come to consolidate them by sound organization. A series of local risings threatened the unity of the Achaemenid possessions. It was no time for clemency, and all the rebel leaders were executed. In the monumental bas-relief sculpted for Darius at Behistun, he is shown under the winged symbol of Ahura-Mazda, marching ahead of two officers and planting his foot on a rebel. There are nine other rebels with their hands tied behind their backs and ropes round their necks (the last, who wears a pointed cap, was added after the others to commemorate a victory over the Scythians). A trilingual inscription recounts the victory of the "King of Kings".

Not content with consolidating Cambyses' empire, Darius enlarged it. There is no doubt that he was responsible for the conquest of the Indian satrapy – not mentioned at Behistun – which corresponds to present-day Sind. For the first time the East really achieved unity. The Persian empire included Egypt and Cyrenaica and reached as far as Turkestan and India. It had a choice of expanding towards the east or west. Darius chose Europe, and after some initial successes he suffered his first setback in Greece (490 B.C.)

at the battle of Marathon. A vital victory for the Greeks, it was an unimportant reverse for the Persians. Pasargadae had become too remote for a capital, though it continued to be a religious centre, and the Emperors were crowned there right up to the end of the empire. Susa took its place as the political and administrative capital. The old Elamite town was splendidly situated for this purpose. The Persian Gulf, giving access to Egypt and India, was only some eighty miles away. The Tigris provided an easy link with Babylon. A citadel and royal palace rose on the acropolis (in the reign of Artaxerxes I the great palace was burnt down and a smaller royal residence was built at the southern end of the town pending the completion of a new palace; all the fragments of bas-reliefs found at Susa come from this small palace).

The work was barely finished when Darius decided to erect a new capital in the heart of the empire, at the spot where Fars now stands: Persepolis, the City of the Persians.[82] This was the impressive setting for the most solemn ceremony of the year: at the spring equinox delegations from the whole empire came to render homage to the King of Kings. Persepolis was a safe town where all the offerings of the vassal peoples could be securely amassed. "There was no imperial form of worship, but the fact that the king was placed on the throne by the will of Ahura-Mazda, the great god and creator, gave the Persian world a sort of unity. Everything in Persepolis was built to exalt national feeling and with a view to the ceremonies held there each year at the beginning of spring ... Under the aegis of Ahura-Mazda... in the presence of the King of Kings, the master nations – the Persians and Medes – watched the procession and the presentation of the offerings that were laid by all the nations of the vast empire at the foot of the throne as tokens of faithfulness and loyalty."[83]

Achaemenid art reached its peak at this period; Persian power was at its height, and until Alexander's lightning campaign the empire continued to base its existence on the foundations laid and consolidated by Cyrus, Cambyses, and Darius. Xerxes (486–465 B.C.) failed in his attempt to regain a foothold in Greece, and the age of expansion was over. Artaxerxes I (465–423) was a weakling. Under Darius II signs of decadence appeared in the form of intrigues and scandals, and rebellions broke out in Sardis, Media, and Egypt. In the reign of his eldest son, Artaxerxes II (404–359 B.C.), the Persian empire grew still weaker: what better evidence is there of this than the famous retreat of the ten thousand

Greek mercenaries who – after the massacre of their leaders – were able to return to their country through Armenia without being molested? Egypt proclaimed its independence, and was allowed to do so without any attempt at reconquest. A revolt of the satrapies shook the empire to its foundations.

Under Artaxerxes III (359–338) Persia tried to pull itself together. The king was obstinate and cruel: he put down the rebellions most resolutely and reconquered Egypt, but he died at the hands of a poisoner and the empire did not long survive him. In the West, new powers were emerging, and the Persians underestimated the danger of Macedonia. When Alexander crossed the Dardanelles with a small army, Darius III ordered that he should be captured and sent to Susa. But the Persian army entrusted with this operation was beaten at the battle of the Granicus. One town after another fell to the enemy. The King of Kings lost his illusions. Having failed to defend the lines of the Tigris and Euphrates, he attempted to buy off his adversaries who refused to bargain over what they were certain of capturing. At Gaugamela, in the foothills of the Assyrian mountains, the Achaemenid empire finally collapsed, and Darius fled to Ecbatana. Susa surrendered without resistance. Whether by accident or design, Persepolis was set on fire. Darius was stabbed by a satrap in the north-east of the plateau, near Damghan.

Achaemenid architecture

Considering the political and religious principles that secured the stability and coherence of the Persian empire for more than two centuries, it is clear that Achaemenid architecture was above all monarchical. Mazdaism forbade the use of temples, so architecture found its chief outlet in the glorification of the monarchy. The basic building was the royal palace. Pasargadae, the "camp of the Persians", was well named. It was indeed more like a camp than a true palace, a camp that extended for a mile and a half. When Cyrus established his residence there, Pasargadae "consisted of little more than a few royal buildings erected in a walled-in park and surrounded – according to the time of year – by a greater or smaller number of tents and flocks".[84] The artificial terrace dominating the enclosure had, however, been built by then, probably in the reign of Cambyses I. It is now called Takht-i-Suleiman, i.e., the throne of Solomon. It consists of a core of rough masonry contained in a framework of large stone blocks (some more than 15 feet long) laid together without mortar. Inside the enclosure were the ceremonial buildings, probably standing at some distance from one another. The remains of ponds and canals suggest that the buildings were intentionally set apart in the middle of gardens; the Greeks mention the garden surrounding Cyrus' tomb.

The excavations of 1949 and 1950[85] have cleared the monumental entrance in the southeast corner of the enclosure. This took the form of a building comprising a pillared hall and two annexes. Two rows of four pillars supported the roof of the great hall. The main door is flanked by two winged bulls on the inside and two bulls with human heads on the outside, all four clearly of Assyrian manufacture. The doors opening on the long sides have not been preserved except for the embrasure of one: a pillar decorated with a bas-relief after which the whole ensemble has been named the "palace of the stele". This stele, which probably dates from the middle of the 6th century B.C., is 9 feet high. It shows a protective winged genius dressed in the long Elamite garment and crowned with an Egyptian-style tiara. Until the 19th century, there was a trilingual (neo-Babylonian, neo-Elamite and Old Persian) inscription: "I, Cyrus, the King, the Achaemenid (built)." The text has now disappeared, but copies preserved by travellers have survived. Two hundred yards farther on was a large audience hall of which only one very slender column survives – whence the name "palace of the column". This large raised hall was surrounded on three sides by a triple portico, while the fourth side was enclosed by two corner rooms. Here we find the prototype of many Achaemenid columns: the base, a square plinth of black stone, is surmounted by a white fluted torus from which rises a smooth white shaft, topped by an impost in the form of a double *protome* of lions or bulls. Such imposts were undoubtedly a direct continuation of the fork-shaped pieces of wood by which beams were held in place.[86] Some distance away is a second palace – some say Cyrus' residence, others a building for ceremonial receptions.[87] This second palace, which was flanked by two porticos, contained some small rooms built of unfired bricks whose purpose remains uncertain. About a mile to the west of the terrace was a building of which very little has survived (a single wall that belonged to a square tower, in freestone). It is easy to reconstruct the tower since the temple of Naqsh i-Rustam is a replica of it. Finally, to the south stood the Meshhed i-Madar-i-Suleiman, the Tomb of Solomon's Mother, i.e., the tomb of Cyrus the Great. It is a fine stone building. On a base with six steps stands a burial chamber with a rather low door in the north side. The limestone blocks are carefully finished, put together without mortar, and assembled with precision. The somewhat heavy top is shaped like a double-pitched roof. It is an impressive ensemble, 35 feet high, the base alone being more than 16 feet high. From the general appearance and from the technique of the stonecutting, R.D. Barnett concludes that this building is related to those of Urartu, and that the Medes served as intermediaries.[88] This certainly seems much closer to the truth than theories linking it with ziggurats such as that at Choga-Zambil.

Persepolis

As Pasargadae had become too small, Cyrus decided to transfer the capital to a more convenient site – that of Persepolis, below the Kuh-i-Rahmat, the Mountain of Grace. The terrace on which the citadel was built is partly artificial and partly cut out of the mountain, and covers 32 acres. It has been attributed to Cyrus, but the buildings were the work of Darius I, Xerxes I, and Artaxerxes I. This was the scene of the magnificent New Year's Festival. Delegations from the whole empire came to Persepolis, surrounding it with their tents. On New Year's Day the great of the kingdom ascended the two flights of stairs leading to a landing, from which they converged on the upper terrace. The steps were wide and low, and horsemen could ride up them without difficulty. At the top of the staircase the guests arrived at Xerxes' monumental door which was decorated with two pairs of bulls with human heads. Through this door they came to the upper platform above which were the residential and ceremonial palaces of the Achaemenid kings, the Treasury (excavated by American archaeologists between 1934 and 1939), and the military buildings. There was, first of all, the great audience hall of Darius and Xerxes (the foundation texts, now in the Museum of Tehran, clearly ascribe the building to them), the Apadana, more than 65 feet high and 198 feet long. The pillared hall was enclosed by four corner towers. On the north and east sides are two splendid double flights of stairs leading to the interior. In the corners are carvings of lions overcoming bulls, symbolizing the triumph of Good over Evil. On the back wall, which covers the base of the Apadana, is a relief showing the procession that constituted the first part of the ceremony. It includes the host of the Immortals, the Persian Guards in their spreading garments, and tribute-bearers from the twenty-three countries that were subject to the empire: Lydians, Cilicians, Babylonians, Gandarians, Bactrians, etc. Each delegation is separated from the next by a tree, no doubt similar to those Darius had planted on the terrace. Dignitaries who were entitled to render homage to the king approached the great hall by the north staircase. The King of Kings entered by the east staircase, and then watched the procession from the terrace in front of the pillared hall. When it was over, the king and the dignitaries left the Apadana and went to the Tripylon, a small building with three doors. The embrasures of the south and north doors are decorated with bas-reliefs showing the king followed by his servants, one of whom is carrying a fly swat, another a parasol. After the banquet, which was held in the palace of Darius, and later in that of his son Xerxes, the king went back through the Tripylon to the throne room, the hall with a hundred columns which was completed by Darius' grandson, Artaxerxes I. In this hall was held the ceremony of homage which is depicted on the reliefs in the embrasures of the entrance. The king – with the heir-apparent behind him – was seated on a throne carried by representatives of the peoples of the empire. He was shielded by a baldaquin surmounted by the symbol of Ahura-Mazda. One after the other the delegations laid their offerings at his feet. Reliefs on the walls show the "Royal Hero" fighting the forces of evil – the dimensions of the building alone were enough to daunt them. The roof was supported by ten rows of ten columns, of which the bases have survived. The hall was 82 yards long and 30 feet high. When the delegates had deposited their offerings, they went out by the Door of Xerxes.[89] A group of buildings in the southeast corner of the terrace comprised the Royal Treasury. Two further buildings should be noted. A residential palace, the *tatchara* of Darius, stood to the west of the terrace. The name of Darius is repeated over and over again on the window frames. The building is not very large, which suggests that it was lived in only in times of need. The other palace, the *hadish* of Xerxes, not far from the *tatchara*, is on a larger scale. It consists of a vast pillared hall, flanked to the west and east by various rooms. It was undoubtedly a ceremonial palace, probably used for distinguished visitors.

A common feature of these Achaemenid buildings, as we have seen, is the vast pillared hall. Achaemenid architects certainly did not invent it, but they exploited its possibilities to the full by using long beams of Lebanon cedar instead of stone lintels. Thanks to the lightness of the wood, 36 columns, spaced out at intervals of 10 yards, were enough to support the ceiling of the Apadana. The columns of the porticos still taper upwards for some 60 feet. These columns were the most original feature of Persian architecture. The foundation texts tell us that Greeks and Lydians were entrusted with cutting them: "The stone columns which were shaped here were brought from a village called Abiradu in Elam. The stone-cutters were Ionians and Sardians."[90] But the Achaemenid columns were not mere copies of Greek works. The bases – often bell-shaped and decorated with leaves or flowers – and the slender, almost disproportionately long shafts owe little to Greece. At Persepolis a wealth of decorative motifs – garlands and hanging leaves – were interposed between the shaft and the capital. The imposts with double *protomes* of animals are purely Achaemenid: for example the *protomes* of bulls on the portico of the Apadana, reminiscent of those on the monumental door of the terrace, the *protomes* of human-headed bulls on the columns of the Tripylon. There are also imposts decorated with horned bulls, and two *protomes* of griffins have been found on unfinished imposts[91] that were never used.

Naqsh i-Rustam

Some three miles from Persepolis, is a sanctuary that pre-dates the Achaemenid period. Some thousand years previously the Elamites had already sculpted a bas-relief there, setting it apart as a sacred place. Under the Achaemenids it was both a sanctuary and a burial ground. In the steep cliff dominating the site are four hypogea containing the tombs of Darius, Xerxes, Artaxerxes I, and Darius II. These four tombs follow the same model: a cruciform façade, the horizontal arm comprising four embedded columns that frame a door. The imposts of the columns are directly influenced by those of Persepolis. The upper part of the vertical arm is decorated with bas-reliefs showing the representatives of the subject peoples upholding the king and Ahura-Mazda on a dais. The tomb of Darius was the first building of its kind. It can be identified by a trilingual inscription.

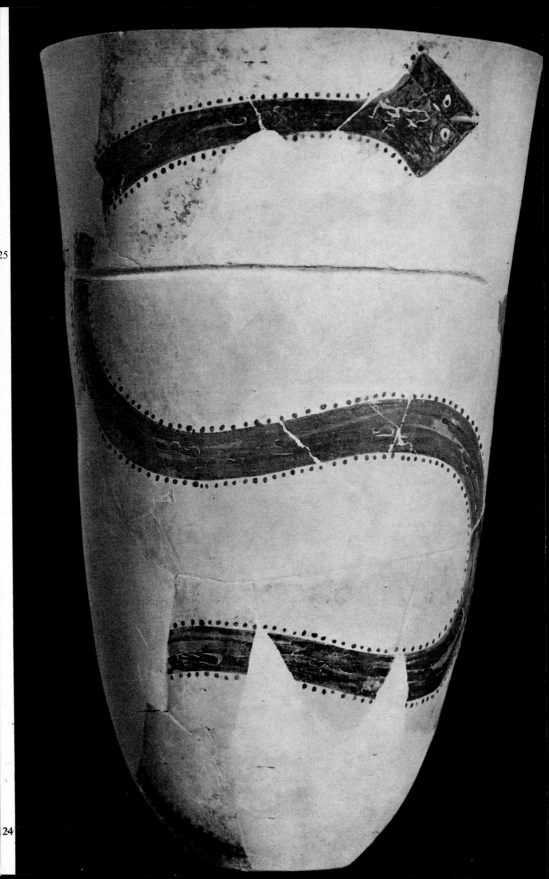

128

132

133

135

136

The funerary chamber comprises three rows of shafts cut in the rock. The whole is extremely impressive, with a façade 74 feet high. The three other hypogea are identical. Do these tombs show that the Achaemenid princes were not strict Zoroastrians? Mazdaism forbade burial as well as cremation for fear of polluting earth or fire. Bodies were simply laid out on a mountain so that birds of prey could strip off the flesh. But the Achaemenid princes were too eclectic to be confined within the bounds of a single religion. It is known, for example, that Cyrus was a devotee of Marduk. Very little is known of Mazdaism in its original form, however, and it is difficult to draw any very definite conclusion from the existence of the rock tombs of Naqsh i-Rustam. In front of the tomb of Artaxerxes is a quadrangular tower, the *Ka'ba i-Zardusht,* the Kaaba of Zoroaster, resembling the collapsed one at Pasargadae.[92] Built of well-bonded limestone blocks, it stands on a triple terrace; it is reinforced with pillars at the corners and decorated with blind windows in black stone. The interior contains a rather small room closed by two swing-doors (slabs turning on sockets, still in place). This building which probably dates from the reign of Darius I, may originally have been a provisional tomb but soon became a temple. Some scholars – for example, the English Orientalist W.B. Henning – think that it was intended for archives. Others – for example, the Swedish scholar S. Wikander – believe that it was a temple of Anahita, the goddess of water and fertility. Ghirshman simply regards it as "one of those temples that sheltered the eternal fire".[93]

Achaemenid architecture was obviously not wholly original. Attempts have been made to analyse what it owed to Egypt, to Elam, Babylon, Assur, and Ionia. But what art is ever wholly original? No art is ever born of nothing. The synthesis obtained by the Persian architects was neither plagiarism nor imitation, but original in itself as an expression of the Persians' genius for adaptation as well as their creative spirit. They achieved a harmonious fusion of the whole Oriental past, bringing it to a climax. Achaemenid architecture had no successors. The basic feature of Parthian architecture was the vault, not the pillared hall. The extraordinary combination that produced Achaemenid architecture was unique. Its love of harmony and lightness is reminiscent of Greece, but its aims had nothing Hellenic about them. It was a sumptuous, solemn, imposing architecture that fulfilled a clear function, a royal architecture with the sole purpose of exalting the monarchy. Greek humanity, movement, and freedom were completely alien to it, and it remained purely Asiatic and Oriental. "When the royal power suddenly collapsed, the art it had created and supported collapsed with it."[94]

Achaemenid sculpture

Achaemenid sculpture has often been compared with that of Assyria. The principle is the same: friezes sculpted at the bottom of walls or in window recesses. But if the formula was identical, its application was very different. The Assyrian frieze was purely decorative. The Assyrian sculptor was obsessed by a minute – almost excessive – realism. His crowded, vigorous reliefs were stone archives, meant to be studied in detail. Nothing stands out, no guiding line emerges from the mass of detail. "The Iranian sculptor," on the other hand, "had learnt that a work of art calls for omissions and that a decoration that is an end in itself is not decorative."[95] His friezes had an architectural as well as a decorative role, since they were intended to emphasize the lines of the buildings they adorned. Achaemenid sculpture was an art of repetition. It has been accused of monotony, but we must remember that we can no longer see these works as they were originally. Some figures in the bas-reliefs were painted, others were enlivened by metal ornaments of which nothing remains except the holes in which they were fixed. These sculptures today appear smooth, almost gentle, but must have produced quite a violent effect at the time. The colours in which they were painted would probably seem loud to us now. But it should be remembered that the Parthenon was also painted and probably altogether lacked the sumptuous whiteness we admire today. There has been much speculation about the relationship between Achaemenid art and Greek art, and with good reason. The Achaemenid rulers of the 5th century B.C. were familar with Greek works, as is shown by the splendid statue of Penelope (second half of the 5th century), which was found in the Treasury at Persepolis in 1938 and is now in the Museum of Tehran. The Charter of Susa mentions the co-operation of Greek craftsmen. But did the Greek influence go beyond a simple technical contribution? The genius of Pasargadae, the first known example of Achaemenid sculpture, is an example of Persian art before it was influenced by Greece. The figure is flat, and all the details are on one plane. It is a shallow relief in an obviously Assyrian style, set against its background like a cut-out silhouette. An analysis of this work shows only strictly Oriental features. "There is no modelling of the limbs through the clothing, and the long fringed shawl-like gown recalls those worn by the courtiers of Sargon of Assyria. The four wings... are also known in Assyria. The beard, on the other hand, is short and round, after the Persian fashion. Upon the cap... is placed the most elaborate of the divine crowns of Egypt. This may be copied directly from imported Egyptian bronzes or from Phoenician work."[96]

Subsequently Achaemenid sculptors learnt how to show rounded forms and to convey figures in depth. The representation of clothes in particular owed its finest achievements to Greek influence. Some of the reliefs at Pasargadae and Persepolis used the technique of the stylized flowing garment, of which there are many examples in archaic Greek statuary. This explains the convention by which "The loose garments of the Persians are arranged in stacked folds with zigzag edges. On the outer side of the sleeve, when seen in profile, the stacked folds are obliquely placed with a zigzag edge in one direction: in the lower part of the garment a bunch of vertical folds, symmetrically stacked... with a zigzag edge running up and down."[97] This convention was used in Greece until the beginning of the 5th century B.C. Nevertheless, the Hellenic influence remained purely technical. The Achaemenid rulers restricted the role of their Greek artists to that of mere executants, for – unlike the Greeks – the Achaemenids aimed at an exclusively monarchical art with a specific political purpose. Just as Persian power dominated the whole Orient, but not Greece, Achaemenid art was a synthesis of the art of the Orient and its spirit was poles apart from that of Greek art. The basic theme of Achaemenid sculpture was the king. In it, the composite monsters – winged or scorpion-tailed – that were taken directly from Assyrian art are vanquished by the Royal Hero. The king – often likened to a god – is everywhere: he is shown enthroned, advancing, triumphant. The whole of Persian iconography was focused on him. It showed his servants, his soldiers, and his subjects. At Behistun he is shown lording it over his fettered enemies, at Persepolis slaying monsters. Usually portrayed in the ample robe of the Medes – majestic in its simplicity – he is truly the King of Kings whom the Greeks regarded as a worthy adversary and not as a contemptible barbarian. He could proclaim in an inscription:

"Think how many different lands King Darius held! Look at the image of those who uphold my throne and you will recognize them. And you will learn that the lance of the Persian has penetrated far, that the Persian has fought far from Persia". Nevertheless, Persian art has a place for narrative, and is not a simple repetition of stereotyped themes. The procession of the tribute-bearers at Persepolis is tremendously varied and alive. We can easily recognize, from a number of details, to which people each bearer belonged. This was by no means a cold inhuman type of art.

The Achaemenid enamelled brick panels are justly famous as examples of a richly royal art. The best known show a procession of the archers – bare-headed, their curly hair held in place by head-bands – of the King of Kings. They are dressed in sumptuously embroidered long garments and hold their lances in front of them with both hands. On their shoulders they carry bows and huge quivers. Other panels show more or less imaginary animals: winged griffins, composite animals with wings, ram's horns and lion's jaws, or roaring lions with lashing tails. The colours in all these panels range from green to yellow, from white to maroon.

Persian artists were also very skilful in the so-called "minor arts". They produced an outstanding collection of animal figurines. One of the finest examples is the winged ibex in the Louvre. It was used as a handle on a vase and was made of partially gilded bronze; there is a matching handle in the Berlin Museum. Here we have a truly Iranian subject treated in a way that show a definite Greek influence. "The spreading wings that enlarge the space round the ibex have nothing Oriental about them, for in Oriental art space was usually as restricted as possible and figures were presented compactly."[98] This work of unsurpassed grace and lightness is thought to date from the first half of the 4th century B.C. It is a magnificent end-product of an art that excelled in both the spectacular and the simple, without ever degenerating into the colossal or the whimsical.

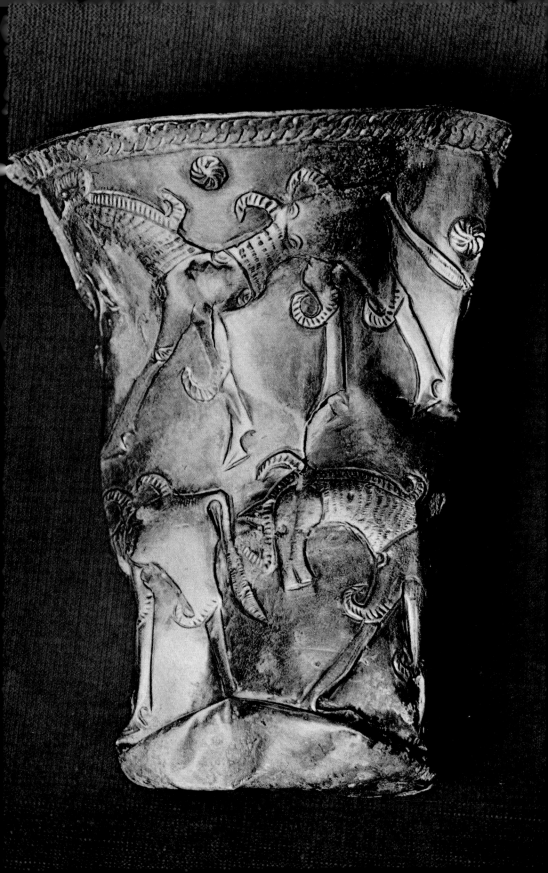

SOME PROBLEMS

III

While it is too early to make a precise assessment of archaeological research in Iran, we can formulate some of the main problems it has raised.

First of all there are the problems connected with prehistory. On most sites in the Orient and Greece the existence of pre-pottery neolithic civilizations has been noted. Very ancient farming villages were found in Mesopotamia after the Second World War, not in the plain proper but on the low hills that overlook it. R. Braidwood recognized the oldest phase on the site of Muallafat, north-east of Iraq, in 1955 (Mission of the Oriental Institute of Chicago).[99] Braidwood's excavations at Qalaat Jarmo some years previously had provided an opportunity to study a dwelling dated *c.* 5000 B.C.[100] by the Carbon 14 method. The implements were still entirely of stone, although there was agriculture (millstones and sickle parts), and animals were domesticated (bones of sheep and cows). The dwellings were of puddled clay, but no pottery was found at the oldest of the eight known levels. Jarmo was still at the pre-pottery stage. Potsherds appeared only at a higher level. Outside Mesopotamia this phase of development has also been observed at Tell es-Sultan (Jericho) by Miss K. Kenyon. In the so-called Pre-Pottery Neolithic Levels A and B there is abundant evidence of the presence of a fairly advanced agricultural community. But pottery had not yet come into use. It is not known if there was a similar pre-pottery neolithic phase in Iran. The oldest known sites, such as Tepe Sarab, already have pottery.[101] The evidence for Iran is not yet complete.

The proto-Elamite civilization that developed in Susiana raises the problem of its precise relations with Sumer. Was there a parallel development of the proto-Elamite and Sumerian civilizations? Did one influence the other and, if so, how and to what extent? In some fields Elam was probably ahead, especially in metallurgy. This is hardly surprising since copper was much more easily accessible in Elam than in the plain. The equivalents of many Sumerian tools are found at Susa in a more archaic form. On the whole, metal-working developed earlier at Susa than at Sumer. Similarly, Susiana created its own script, the pictographic system of the proto-Elamite tablets. But this system was finally replaced by the Mesopotamian cuneiform.[102] Without suggesting that the civilization of Susa I was a forerunner of the Ubaid civilization of Sumer, we can still, with G. Childe, consider it as a culture collateral with that of Ubaid, springing from the same south-Iranian background.[103] The proto-Elamite script was not borrowed from Sumer but invented at Susa itself. However, a much closer analysis of the relationships between the two cultures is needed. What was happening in the field of gem-engraving?

Another unsolved problem is raised by the grey, or polished black, pottery series. As we have seen, there was a change in pottery in northern Iran at the beginning of the 3rd millennium B.C. Between one settlement and the next, painted pottery became rare and a grey or grey-black pottery appeared whose colour and shape bore no resemblance to anything occuring previously on the Iranian plateau. This pottery is found at Tepe Hissar III B-C and at Tureng Tepe. The presence on the latter site, in a layer of grey pottery, of plano-convex bricks suggests that the layer dates from the 3rd millennium. First of all, the grey pottery raises the problem of this provenance. We know very little of the origins of this new culture or of the people who brought it to Iran. It shows a certain break with Chalcolithic pottery and this almost certainly indicates a settlement of new-comers, whose origin might be sought in the region of the northern steppes, towards Russian Turkestan. What were the relationships between the different groups using grey pottery? This technique spread gradually in the north-east and north-west of the Iranian plateau (Yanik Tepe, Geoy Tepe), and even penetrated as far as Cappadocia (Kul Tepe, Alishar, etc.). There are obvious points of resemblance between the grey Iranian pottery and the grey Anatolian pottery, especially a predilection for outlines imitated from metal vases. But does a relationship between styles necessarily mean a relationship between peoples? Again, if such a relationship existed, are we already concerned with Indo-European peoples? Some experts think so. Finally, grey pottery is again found in north-west and central Iran at the end of the 2nd millennium B.C.: it is found in Necropolis A at Siyalk; the same colour and metal-type shapes are found at Khurvin, fifty miles from Tehran, and the same pottery is found at Hasanlu in Azerbaijan, where American excavations have brought to light a very fragile black variety, with thin sides, in which the resemblance to metal is emphasized by grooves on the belly.[104] But there is a gap of a millennium between the two series of pottery (grey and grey-black) and this still remains unexplained. Many sites appear to have been more or less completely abandoned a little after the beginning of the 2nd millennium. The same thing has been observed at sites in the Turcoman plain, at Tepe Hissar, Siyalk, and Yanik Tepe. It is certain that Susa experienced an eclipse until the revival of the Elamite kingdom.

This revival more or less coincided with the resurrection of several abandoned sites (for example Hasanlu and Siyalk). Tepe Hissar, on the other hand, remained deserted. Other sites, such as Yanik Tepe, were reoccupied only much later. Tureng Tepe was sparsely inhabited in the Iron Age. It is not known why these sites were abandoned at the beginning of the 2nd millennium. Was there a change in the climate? It is difficult to visualize a change in climate that would make the inhabitants leave within such a short space of time. Moreover, Tureng Tepe lies in a region that is now very fertile. Was it due to some political catastrophe? But, if so, would this not have been caused by new invaders, who would immediately have reoccupied the sites? There is no trace of any general destruction.

The passing of Iran from the Bronze Age to the Iron Age at the beginning of the 1st millennium raises further questions for the archaeologist. The period covering the end of the Bronze Age and the first centuries of the Iron Age still remains obscure in many respects. There is as yet no complete agreement on the character and date of Necropoles A and B at Siyalk. Does the latter prove the arrival and settlement of the "Iranian" peoples, as Ghirshman claims? Similar problems relating to more or less the same period are raised by the Luristan bronzes. What was their exact date and their provenance? The appellation "Luristan" does not always cover objects of the same kind, and many of them are in fact Susan. In the present state of research it is difficult to attribute these bronzes to a specific people. Were they Kassite? Were they "Iranian" in the true sense of the word? What relation is there between these bronzes and those of the Caucasus or the steppes?

Finally, the Achaemenid period which seems to be the best known and most closely studied, still needs much examination. In this civilization born of a synthesis, it is essential to evaluate what was the actual Persian contribution and what was simply taken from one Oriental civilization or another. The Achaemenids, who were empire-building sovereigns, would of neccessity have had close relations with all the civilizations of the Near East. To which did they owe most – to Urartu, to Assyria, to Ionian Greece, or to Egypt? Which features were taken from the artistic *Koinë* of all Western Asia in which Syria–Phoenicia played a leading part? Did the Persians simply assemble disparate pieces or did they act as true catalysts? Such are the main lines of modern research in the field of Iranian archaeology. These are the chief problems awaiting satisfactory solution. There is still a great deal of uncertainty. But the field is fairly new, and the labourers – in relation to the vastness of the task – are relatively few.

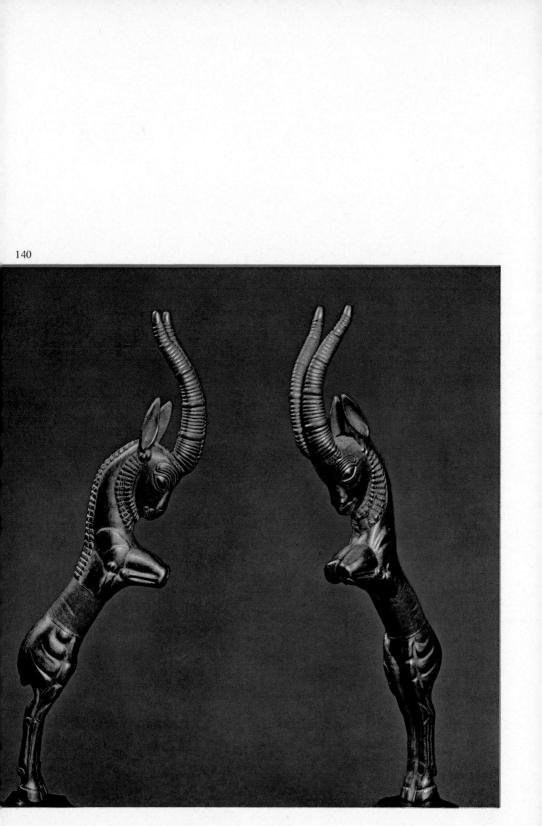

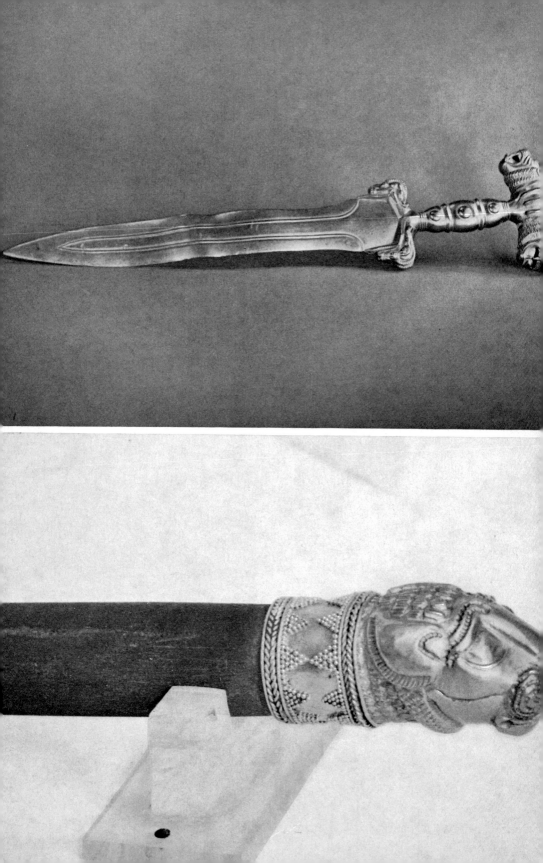

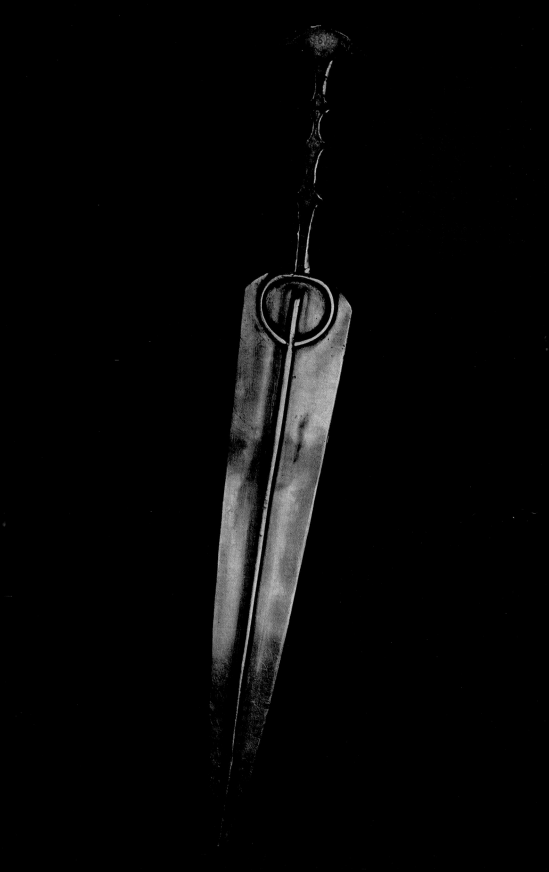

NOTES

[1] R. Ghirshman, *Fouilles de Sialk I*, page 65 sq. pl. XLII, XLIII.

[2] The most recently found objects proving this spread of Aramaic include three items in the Foroughi collection with Aramaic inscriptions that permit them to be dated *c.* 800, 711 and 600 B.C. respectively. These are a jug and two bowls from Luristan. The inscriptions illustrate the spread of Aramaic through the Zagros in the Assyrian era. M. Dupont-Sommer, Professor at the College de France made a report on these inscriptions to the Academie des Inscriptions et Belles-Lettres, on 2nd October 1964. They will shortly be published in *Iranica Antiqua*.

[3] E. Herzfeld, *Iran in the Ancient East*, London and New York 1941, page 7.

[4] Marcel Dieulafoy. *Les Antiquités de Suse découvertes et rapportées par la Mission Dieulafoy* (1884–86), Paris 1913.
   Jeanne Dieulafoy. *A Suse. Journal des Fouilles*. Paris 1888.

[5] A. Parrot, *Archéologie Mésopotamienne*, Paris 1946. Vol. I, page 171.

[6] An analysis of the contents of all these volumes will be found in A. Parrot, *Archéologie Mésopotamienne* vol. I, page 258 et seq.

[7] A. Godard, Bronzes du Luristan, *Ars Asiatica*, Van Oest, Paris 1931.

[8] Erich Schmidt, The Second Holmes Expedition to Luristan, in *Bulletin of the American Institute for Iranian Art and Archaeology V.* (1938).

[9] G. Contenau and R. Ghirshman, *Fouilles de Tépé Giyan près de Néhavend*, 1931 and 1932. Louvre, Department of Oriental Antiquities, archaeological series, vol. III. Paris 1935.

[10] G. Contenau, *Manuel d'Archéologie Orientale depuis les Origines jusqu'à l'époque d'Alexandre*, Paris 1927–47.

[11] R. Ghirshman, *Fouilles de Sialk, près de Kashan*, 1933, 1934, 1937, vols. I and II, Paris 1939.

[12] F. Wulsin, Excavations at Tureng-Tepe, Suppl. to the *Bulletin of the American Institute for Persian Art and Archaeology*, vol. II No 1b (March 1932).

[13] A. Langsdorff and D. E. McCown, Tall i-Bakun A, Season of 1932, University of Chicago, *Oriental Institute Publications LIX* (1942).

[14] Results published in E. F. Schmidt, *Excavations at Tepe Hissar-Damghan*, Philadelphia 1937; this work was preceded by a preliminary report, "Tepe Hissar excavations, 1931", in *Museum Journal*, XXIII, 4, 1933.

[15] T.J. Arne, *Excavations at Shah Tepe, Iran*, Stockholm 1945.

[16] Jean Deshayes, Rapport préliminaire sur les deux premières campagnes de fouilles à Tureng-Tépé, in *Syria*, XL, 1963.

[17] Sir Mortimer Wheeler, *Archaeology from the Earth*, Oxford, Clarendon Press, 1954, page 1.

[18] "By demolishing the old walls – that have no interest – we find the foundation texts", J. de Morgan, *Les Recherches archéologiques, leur but et leur procédé*, Paris 1906, page 37.

[19] G. Contenau, *Manuel d'Archéologie Orientale*, vol. IV. page 1720.

[20] J. de Morgan, *Les Recherches archéologiques*, page 1.

[21] J. de Morgan, *Les Recherches archéologiques*, page 35.

[22] A. Parrot, *Archéologie Mésopotamienne*, vol. II, page 27.

[23] *Histoire et Travaux de la Délégation en Perse du Ministère de l'Instruction Publique*, 1897–1905, page 50.

[24] A. Leroi-Gourhan, in *Etudes Archéologiques*, Paris 1963, page 49.

[25] A. Leroi-Gourhan, in *Etudes Archéologiques*, Paris 1963, page 54.

[26] W.F. Albright, *L'Archéologie de la Palestine*, Paris 1955, page 7.

[27] Sir Mortimer Wheeler, *Archaeology from the Earth*, page 49.

[28] The Akkadian tablets of Susa, Malamir and Liyan (Busbire) should also be mentioned.

[29] V. Gordon Childe, *Man Makes Himself*, London 1941.

[30] H. Read, *The Meaning of Art*, Penguin Books, 1964, (new edition), pages 32 and 33.

[31] The potter's work has often been regarded as the symbol of creation, and Jehovah created Man in the manner of a potter. It is written, "And the Lord God formed man of the dust of the ground", ('t h'dm 'phr mn h'dmh – thus the pun on the word man, 'dm, taken from 'dhm, the red earth). Genesis 2.7. The example of the potter is used by Jeremiah (18.2) to describe someone who moulds something to his will: "Arise, and go down to the potter's house, and there I will cause thee to hear my words. Then I went down to the potter's house, and, behold, he wrought a work on the wheels. And the vessel that he made of clay was marred in the hand of the potter; so he made it again another vessel, as seemed good to the potter to make it. Then the word of the Lord came to me, saying, O house of Israel, cannot I do with you as this potter?" (Jeremiah 18, 2-6, Authorized Version).
This image of the potter recurs in Jeremiah, the Book of Wisdom, Saint Paul, etc.

[32] A. Leroi-Gourhan, in *Etudes Archéologiques*, Paris 1963, page 56.

[33] R. Ghirshman, *Fouilles de Sialk près de Kashan*, vol. I 1938, vol. II 1939.

[34] Cf. however Braidwood and Howe, *Prehistoric Investigations in Iraqi Kurdistan*, 1960, p. 143: "Ghirshman (1954, p. 29) has claimed that stock breeding is indicated by the Iranian assemblage at Sialk I. ... for bones of domesticated oxen and sheep were found in the remains of period I. The only evidence for this sweeping statement, when one examines the original report (Vaufrey in Ghirshman, *Fouilles de Sialk*, vol. II pp. 195–197) consists of six 'sheep' (possibly goat) teeth and two teeth of bovini ... such a minimum of evidence suggests extreme rarity of cattle in the region. Furthermore, cattle are not recorded from higher levels at Sialk ..."

[35] E. Porada, *Iran Ancien*, Paris 1963, page 16.

[36] Anau, *Explorations in Turkestan, Prehistoric Civilizations of Anau*, by R. Pumpelly, 2 vols., Washington 1908.

[37] E.F. Schmidt, *Excavations at Tepe Hissar, Damghan*, 1931–33, Philadelphia 1937.

[38] D.E. McCown, *The Comparative Stratigraphy of Early Iran*, OIS, 23, 1942.

[39] Cf. Siyalk, page 135, pl. LXIX.

[40] A. Langsdorff and D.E. McCown, Tall i-Bakun A, Season of 1932, University of Chicago, *Oriental Institute Publications* LIX (1942).

[41] E. Pottier, Etudes historiques et chronologiques sur les vases peints de l'Acropole de Suse; in *Mémoires de la Délégation en Perse*, vol. XIII (1912), pages 27–103.

[42] Susa A: *MDP* I, 17; XIII, 33; XXV, 183, 204; XXX, 193–198.

[43] Suggested by E. Porada, *op. cit.*, page 20.

[44] A. Parrot, *Sumer*, Coll. "L'Univers des Formes", Paris 1960, page 61.

[45] Cf. E. Porada, A leonine figure of the protoliterate period in Mesopotamia, in *Journal of the American Oriental Society*, 70 (1950), pages 223–226.

[46] Cf. Jean Deshayes, Rapport préliminaire sur les deux premières campagnes de fouille à Tureng-Tépé, in *Syria XL*, 1963, page 85. See plate on page 97.

[47] R. Ghirshman, *L'Iran des origines à l'Islam*, Paris 1951, page 52.

[48] R. de Mecquenem, Recherches à Choga-Zambil *MMAI*, vol. 33.

[49] See the preliminary report in *Arts Asiatiques* (1954).

[50] In 1959 a plan of all the temples was given in *Arts Asiatiques VI* (1959) pages 260–261, fig. 1.

[51] M. Pézard and E. Pottier, Musée National du Louvre. *Catalogue des Antiquités de la Susiane*, Paris, Musées Nationaux, 1926, No. 232.

[52] J.-E. Gautier, Le Sit Shamshi de Silhak Insusinak, *MDP XII* (1911), pages 143–151.

[53] E. Porada, *Iran Ancien*, page 55.

[54] G. Contenau, *Manuel d'Archéologie Orientale*, vol. II, page 922 (fig. 635).

[55] A. Parrot, *Sumer*, page 332.

[56] Described by G. Lampre in *MDP VIII* (1905), pages 245–250. Cf. M. Pézard and E. Pottier, *op. cit.* Catalogue No 230.

[57] Description of the discovery by R. de Mecquenem in *MDP VII* (1905), pages 131–136.

[58] For example, the collection assembled by J. Coiffard, Ambassador in Tehran, and acquired by the Louvre in 1958. See *Revue du Louvre*, No 1, 1963.

[59] Cf. Erich Schmidt, The Second Holmes Expedition to Luristan, in *Bulletin of the American Institute for Iranian Art and Archaeology V* (1938). See also A.U. Pope, A note on some pottery from the Holmes Luristan Expedition, *idem* 1936, page 120.

[60] A. Godard, Les Bronzes du Luristan, in *Ars Asiatica* XVII, 1931.

[61] A. Godard, *op. cit.*, page 19. In 1931 another traveller was able to visit the north-west of Luristan, and brought back information on the site of the Luristan necropoles: Miss Freya Stark, *The Valley of the Assassins*, London 1934.

[62] A. Godard, *op. cit.*, page 23.

[63] Pierre Amiet, Les Bronzes du Luristan de la collection Coiffard, in *Revue du Louvre*, No 1, 1963.

[64] A. Godard, *L'Art de l'Iran*, Paris 1962, pages 70–71.

[65] Cf. A. Godard, *Bronzes...*, pl. VIII, figs. 16 and 17.

[66] Cf. C.F.A. Schaeffer, *Stratigraphie comparée et chronologie de l'Asie Occidentale*, London 1948, fig. 44, No 6.

[67] R. Ghirshman, *Perse*, Paris 1963, page 42.

[68] J. Deshayes, *Les Outils de Bronze, de l'Indus au Danube* (4th to 2nd millennium), Paris 1960.

[69] R. Ghirshman, *Fouilles de Sialk*, vol. II, page 72.

[70] R. Ghirshman, *Fouilles de Sialk*, vol. II pages 26–27.

[71] R. Ghirshman, *Fouilles de Sialk*, vol. II page 29.

[72] R. Ghirshman, *Fouilles de Sialk*, vol. II page 95.

[73] The approximate dates of the destruction of the citadel have been published in *Archaeology XIII* (1960), 129.

[74] For the myth of Kumarbi see Hans Gustav Güterbock, *Kumarbi, Mythen von churritischen Kronos aus den hetitischen Fragmenten zusammengestellt, übersetzt und erklärt* (Istanbuler Schriften, 16), Zurich-New York, Europaverlag, 1946.

[75] See E.O. Negahbau, The Wonderful Gold Treasure of Marlik; *Illustrated London News*, 28 April 1962.

[76] See H. Samadi, Les découvertes fortuites, in *Arts Asiatiques VI*, 1959.

[77] Cf. Iran, vol. III, p. 83.

[78] A. Godard, *Le Trésor de Ziwiyé (Kurdistan)*, Publications du Service Archéologique de l'Iran, Haarlem, 1950.

[79] Toprak Kale, a Uraturian citadel near Lake Van.

[80] R. Ghirshman, *Perse*, page 124.

[81] At first the Achaemenid state showed consideration for its subject peoples, treating them as allies rather than subjects. Thus in the very year of the capture of Babylon (539) Cyrus permitted the deported Jews to return to Jerusalem and rebuild the Temple; this earned him the gratitude of the Jewish people who hailed him as "the Lord's Anointed". "Thus saith the Lord to his anointed, to Cyrus, whose right hand I have holden, to subdue nations before him ... I will go before thee, and make the crooked places straight ..." (Isaiah, 45, 1–2).

[82] Some archaeologists think that the choice of the site of Persepolis and even the initial work on the terrace were due to Cyrus. A. Godard even suggests the year 540 B.C. (*L'Art de l'Iran*, Paris 1962, page 118). The chief reason put forward in support of this theory is that Darius could not have chosen the site of Persepolis as late as 518 and then built the imposing ensemble of the Terrace, the Tatchara and the Apadana during his reign. Herzfeld's work at Persepolis in 1931 brought to light what the excavators believe to be the foundations of Cambyses' tombs.

[83] R. Ghirshman, *Perse*, page 154.

[84] A. Godard, *L'Art de l'Iran*, page 118.

[85] E. Herzfeld, Bericht über die Ausgrabungen von Pasargadae, 1928, in *Archäologische Mitteilungen aus Iran I* (1929).
   A. Sami, *Pasargadae*, Shiraz 1956.

[86] This is the opinion held by E. Herzfeld, *Iran*, pages 209–211.

[87] E. Herzfeld believes that this second palace was the king's private residence, but R. Ghirshman thinks it was a "place used for the receptions and banquets that followed the audiences" (Ghirshman, *Perse*, page 134).

[88] R.D. Barnett, Persepolis, in *Iraq* XIX (1957) 74.

[89] It seems that the "hall of a hundred columns" – besides being used for the ceremony of homage – was also a meeting place for the army. It was not simply an audience hall (this would have duplicated the function of the Apadana). The reliefs in the hall of a hundred columns are different from those in other buildings: the king's throne, which was traditionally supported by the subject "nations" of the empire, is here upheld by rows of warriors – the army supporting the throne. This vast hall has also been regarded as the meeting place of the famous Immortals.

[90] "Charter of the Palace of Susa", based on the text given by R.G. Kent in *American Oriental Society*, 1950, page 144.

[91] Described by A. Godard in *Illustrated London News*, 2nd January 1954, page 18.

[92] Kurt Erdmann, the German Orientalist and Director of the Museum of West Berlin, has described this building in *Das Iranische Feuerheiligtum*, Leipzig 1941, pages 17–18.

[93] R. Ghirshman, *Perse*, page 230.

[94] A. Godard, *L'Art de l'Iran*, page 137.

[95] A. Godard, *L'Art de l'Iran*, page 128.

[96] H. Frankfort, *The Art and Architecture of the Ancient Orient*, Penguin Books, 1954, page 226.

[97] Gisela M.A. Richter, "Greeks in Persia", in *American Journal of Archaeology*, L (1946) 17.

[98] E. Porada, *Iran ancien*, page 165.

[99] R.J. Braidwood, "The world's first farming villages", in *Illustrated London News*, 28th April 1956, pages 410–411.

[100] R.J. Braidwood, *Antiquity*, XXIV, 1950, pages 190–196.

[101] See R.J. Braidwood, in *Iranica Antiqua I*.

[102] See R. de Mecquenem "Epigraphie Protoélamite" in *MDP*, XXXI.

[103] V. Gordon Childe, *New Light in the Most Ancient East*, London 1934.

[104] R. Dyson, Hasanlu and Early Iran, in *Archaeology* 13 (1960).

BIBLIOGRAPHY

Only the main works of reference are listed below. The works cited have extensive bibliographies which will enable readers to pursue the subject in greater detail.

I) Bibliographies

VANDEN BERGHE, *Archéologie de l'Iran Ancien*, Leiden 1959 contains a bibliography (until 1959) on the art and architecture of Iran.

VANDEN BERGHE AND MUSSCHE, *Bibliographie analytique de l'Assyriologie et de l'Archéologie du Proche-Orient*, vol. I. L'Archéologie, Iran, Leiden 1956.

II) General works

AMIET (P.), *La glyptique mésopotamienne archaïque*, Paris 1961.

CAMERON (G.), *Histoire de l'Iran Antique*, trans. R.-J. Lévy, Paris 1937.

CHILDE (V.-G.), *History of early Iran*, Chicago Ill. 1936.

CONTENAU (G.), *Manuel d'Archéologie Orientale*, Paris, 4 vols. 1927–1947.

DESHAYES (J.), *Les Outils de Bronze, de l'Indus au Danube (IVe au IIe millénaires)*, Paris 1960.

FRANKFORT (H.), *The Art and Architecture of the Ancient Orient*, "The Pelican History of Art", Penguin Books 1954.

GHIRSHMAN (R.), *Perse*, Protoiraniens, Mèdes, Achéménides, Paris 1963. *L'Iran des Origines à l'Islam*, Paris 1951.

GODARD (A.), *L'Art de l'Iran*, Paris 1962.

HERZFELD (E.), *Archaeological History of Iran*, in The Schweich Lectures of the British Academy, 1934, London. *Iran in the Ancient East*. London and New York, Oxford University Press, 1941.

McCOWN (D.E.), *The Comparative Stratigraphy of Early Iran*, in *Studies in Ancient Oriental Civilization* No 23, The Oriental Institute of the University of Chicago 1942. *The Relative Stratigraphy and Chronology of Iran*, in *Relative Chronologies in Old World Archaeology*, Chicago 1954, published by R.W. Ehrich.

PARROT (A.), *Archéologie Mésopotamienne*, 2 vols. Paris 1947–53. *Sumer*, Paris 1960.

POPE (A.U.), *A Survey of Persian Art from prehistoric times to the present*, New York – London 1938.

PORADA (E.), *Iran Ancien*, l'Art à l'époque préislamique, Paris 1963.

SCHAEFFER (C.F.A.), *Stratigraphie comparée et chronologie de l'Asie occidentale (IIIe et IIe millénaires)*, "The Griffith Institute, Ashmolean Museum, Oxford", London, Oxford, University Press, 1948.

STEIN (A.), *An archaeological tour in Ancient Persis*, in *Iraq*, vol. III, part 2, pages 111–226, 1936. *Old Routes of Western Iraq*, London 1940.

III) Sites

GEOY TEPE: T. Burton Brown, *Excavations in Azarbaidjan*, 1948, London 1951.

HASANLU: R.H. Dyson, Hasanlu and Early Iran, in *Archaeology* 13 (1960).

LURISTAN: A. Godard, Les Bronzes du Luristan, in *Ars Asiatica* XVII, 1931.

PERSEPOLIS: E.F. Schmidt, *Persepolis I*, Structures, reliefs, inscriptions, The University of Chicago Oriental Institute Publications, vol. LXVIII, Chicago 1953. *Persepolis II*, Contents of the Treasury and other discoveries, The University of Chicago Oriental Institute Publications, vol. LXIX, Chicago 1957.

SUSA: L. Le Breton, The Early Periods at Susa, Mesopotamian relations, in *Iraq* XIX T1957).
R. de Mecquenem, Catalogue de la céramique peinte susienne conservée au Louvre, *MDP*, vol. XIII (1912).
– Notes sur la céramique peinte archaïque en Perse, *MDP*, vol. XX (1928).
– Fouilles de Suse, 1929–33, *MDP*, vol. XXV (1934).

TELL I-BAKUN: A. Langsdorff and D.-E. McCown, *Tall i-Bakun A*, Season of 1932, University of Chicago, Oriental Institute Publications, LIX (1942).

TEPE GIYAN: G. Contenau and R. Ghirshman, *Fouilles du Tépé Giyan près de Néhavend*, 1931-1932, Musée du Louvre. Département des Antiquités Orientales, Série Archéologique, vol. III, Paris 1935.

TEPE HISSAR: E.-F. Schmidt, *Excavations at Tepe Hissar Damghan*, in Publications of the Iranian Section of the University Museum, The University Museum, Philadelphia (1937).

TEPE SIYALK: R. Ghirshman, *Fouilles de Sialk près de Kashan*, vol. I, Musée du Louvre, Département des Antiquités Orientales, Série Archéologique, vol. IV, Paris 1938.

TURENG TEPE: F. Wulsin, *Excavations at Tureng Tepe near Asterabad* in Supplement to the Bulletin of the American Institute for Persian Art and Archaeology, vol. 2, No 1 b (March 1932).
J. Deshayes, Rapport Préliminaire sur les deux premières campagnes de fouilles à Tureng Tépé, in *Syria* XL, 1963.

ZIWIYEH: A. Godard, Le Trésor de Ziwiyé (Kurdistan), *Publications du service archéologique de l'Iran*, Haarlem 1950.

INDEX

LIST OF ILLUSTRATIONS

37 *Bas-relief at Persepolis. A Persian guard carrying a lance. Achaemenid period. 5th century B.C. (phot. G. Bertin)*

38 *Achaemenid tomb at Naksh-i-Rustam, near Persepolis. (phot. G. Bertin)*

39 *Idem.*

40 *Idem.*

41 *Idem.*

42 *Pasargadae. (phot. G. Bertin)*

43 *Palace of Cyrus at Pasargadae. (phot. G. Bertin)*

44 *Idem.*

45 *Idem.*

46 *Idem.*

47 *Remains of the temple of fire. 6th century B.C. Pasargadae. (phot. G. Bertin)*

48 *Cup with stem, decorated with ibexes and geometrical designs, painted brown. Terracotta. From Hissar I c (Damgham). 3500 B.C. Archaeology Museum, Tehran. (phot. Museum)*

49 *Horse-shaped vase. Yellow-buff terracotta. The polychrome decoration of the harness and saddle-cloth consists of birds on a field with flowers. From Maku (Azerbaijan). 8th–7th century B.C. Archaeology Museum, Tehran. (phot. Museum)*

50 *Horse-shaped terracotta vase. The decoration of the harness and the saddle-cloth is a light brick red on a yellowish-brown background and consists of wild boars and birds. From a Persian Achaemenid village, Susa. 7th century B.C. Archaeology Museum, Tehran. (phot. Museum)*

51 *Cylindrical gold cup decorated with three lions. The bodies, in profile, are embossed, the heads, full face, in the round. From Kalardasht (Mazanderan). 9th century B.C. Archaeology Museum, Tehran. (phot. Museum)*

52 *Gold handle of sharpener, shaped like a gazelle's head. From Hamadan. Achaemenid period. Archaeology Museum, Tehran. (phot. Museum)*

53   *Solid gold rhyton shaped like a gazelle's head. The edge is decorated with several rows of very thin gold wire. From Hamadan. Achaemenid period. Archaeology Museum, Tehran. (phot. Museum)*

54   *Vase shaped like a horned animal. From Gilan. Beginning of the 1st millennium B.C. Archaeology Museum, Tehran. (phot. Museum)*

55   *Vase in the shaped of a stylized humped animal (humped bull or zebu). Terracotta. From Gilan. Beginning of the 1st millennium B.C. Archaeology Museum, Tehran. (phot. Museum)*

56   *Vase in the shape of a stylized humped animal (humped bull or zebu). Terracotta. From Gilan. Beginning of the 1st millennium B.C. Archaeology Museum, Tehran. (photo Museum)*

57   *Ritual vase. Terracotta from Amlash. Beginning of the 1st millennium B.C. Louvre. (phot. Studio Josse)*

58   *Vase in the shape of a stylized humped animal, mounted on wheels (humped bull or zebu). Terracotta. The animal's ears are decorated with gold rings. From Gilan. Beginning of the 1st millennium B.C. Archaeology Museum, Tehran. (phot. Museum)*

59   *Terracotta ram from Susa. Beginning of the 3rd millennium B.C. Louvre. (phot. Studio Josse)*

60   *Pinkish-beige terracotta vase in the shape of an animal. The spout is attached to the body by two handles. From Khurvin. Beginning of the 1st millennium B.C. Archaeology Museum, Tehran. (phot. Museum)*

61   *Silver bull's head (the body has been restored) and small silver bull. Achaemenid period. Archaeology Museum, Tehran. (phot. Museum)*

62   *Capital from Persepolis. 5th century B.C. Archaeology Museum, Tehran. (phot. Museum)*

63   *Capital from the Apadana of Artaxerxes II (404–359 B.C.). Marble. Susa. Louvre. (phot. Studio Josse)*

64   *Painted vase with spout from Necropolis B at Siyalk. 10th–9th century B.C. Archaeology Museum, Tehran. (phot. Museum)*

65 *Terracotta vase with long spout, decorated with two stylized bulls and geometrical designs painted in purplish red. From Siyalk VI. 1000–800 B.C. Archaeology Museum, Tehran. (phot. Museum)*

66 *Painted potsherd, decorated with two ibexes. Tepe Giyan V. Louvre. (phot. Studio Josse)*

67 *Pillar with cuneiform inscription from the audience hall of Cyrus. Pasargadae. (phot. G. Bertin)*

68 *Tomb of Cyrus at Pasargadae. (phot. G. Bertin)*

69 *Fragment from a bas-relief of the fish-god. Palace of Cyrus. Pasargadae. (phot. G. Bertin)*

70 *Silver plaque (chamfer?). Harness or chariot ornament. In the centre, a leaping lion between two stylized trees. From Ziwiyeh (Kurdistan). 7th century B.C. Archaeology Museum, Tehran. (phot. Museum)*

71 *Small recumbent bronze lion with a handle (probably a weight). From Persepolis. Achaemenid period. 5th–4th century B.C. Archaeology Museum, Tehran. (phot. Museum)*

72 *Votive axe decorated with a figure holding a fish. From Luristan. Beginning of the 1st millennium B.C. Archaeology Museum, Tehran. (phot. Museum)*

73 *Ceremonial axe from Luristan. Bronze. Louvre. (phot. Studio Josse)*

74 *Idem.*

75 *Axe shaped like a horse's head. Bronze. From Luristan. Louvre. (phot. Studio Josse)*

76 *Bronze daggers from Luristan. Each weapon was made from a single piece with two tabs folding over a decorative handle of wood or bone. Left: uninscribed dagger. Private collection. Paris. Right: dagger belonging to Marduk-nadin-akhe (end of the 2nd millennium B.C.) Louvre. (phot. Studio Josse)*

77 *Religious object (use unknown) decorated on both sides. Black stone. On the side shown, an eagle with spreading wings is fighting two snakes. On the reverse, the motif of a door-frame is repeated eight times. From Azerbaijan. 3rd millennium B.C. Archaeology Museum, Tehran. (phot. Museum)*

78 *Small bronze animals. From Gilan. Beginning of the 1st millennium B.C. Archaeology Museum, Tehran. (phot. Museum)*

79 *Two small bronze animals, back to back. From Luristan. Beginning of the 1st millennium B.C. Archaeology Museum, Tehran. (phot. Museum)*

80 *Bronze handle of sharpener surmounted by two does. From Luristan. Beginning of the 1st millennium B.C. Archaeology Museum, Tehran. (phot. Museum)*

81 *Goblet. Silver, touched up with electrum. Two rows of decoration: in the upper part, a battle scene, in the lower part a hunting scene. The lip and bottom of the goblet are decorated with stylized flowers. From Hasanlu (Azerbaijan). Beginning of the 1st millennium B.C. Archaeology Museum, Tehran. (phot. Museum)*

82 *Cone-shaped terracotta goblet, decorated with geometrical designs, painted in black on a cream-coloured background. From Tell-i-Bakun, a prehistoric village near Persepolis. c. 3600 B.C. Archaeology Museum, Tehran. (phot. Museum)*

83 *Bronze cauldron lug (?) surmounted by a bull's head. From Persepolis. Achaemenid period. Archaeology Museum, Tehran. (phot. Museum)*

84 *Terracotta figurines. Left, musician (c. 1500 B.C.); right, naked goddess without head or arms (c. 2500 B.C.). From Susa. Archaeology Museum, Tehran. (phot. Museum)*

85 *The Sit Shamshi (detail). Model representing a ceremony, dedicated by Shilak-Inshushinak. Bronze. Middle Elamite (12th century B.C.). Louvre. (phot. Studio Josse)*

86 *Bronze votive axe, decorated with a lion, a seated person and a bird with spreading wings. From Sakiz (Kurdistan). End of the 2nd or beginning of the 1st millennium B.C. Archaeology Museum, Tehran. (phot. Museum)*

87 *Bronze figurine from Luristan. Beginning of the 1st millennium B.C. Musée d'Art et d'Histoire, Geneva. (phot. J. Arlaud)*

88 *Head of a bearded man. Terracota from Susa. Elamite style. Beginning of the 1st millennium B.C. Louvre. (phot. Studio Josse)*

89 *Statuettes from the store of Inshushinak at Susa. Gold and silver. Middle Elamite (13th–12th century B.C.). Louvre. (phot. Studio Josse)*

90 *Bronze statuette of a standing deity dressed in a long robe and girded with a sword. A quiver is fixed by a strap to the back. A neo-Babylonian cuneiform inscription on the robe dates from 600 B.C. The statuette itself is older and probably dates from the 1st millennium B.C. From Luristan. Archaeology Museum, Tehran. (phot. Museum)*

91 *Gold breastplate decorated with two rows of mythological scenes: processions of composite creatures moving towards a stylized tree of life in the centre. From Ziwiyeh (Kurdistan). 7th century B.C. Archaeology Museum, Tehran. (phot. Museum)*

92 *Gold bracelet. Two pairs of crouching lion cubs decorate the centre while there is a lion's head at each end. From Ziwiyeh (Kurdistan). 7th century B.C. Archaeology Museum, Tehran. (phot. Museum)*

93 *Statue (detail) of Napir Asu, wife of the Elamite King Untash-Huban. Bronze. About 1234–1227 B.C. Louvre. (phot. Studio Josse)*

94 *Cylindrical vase with a handle in the shape of two small standing persons dressed in kaunakes. Carved bitumen. The upper edge is decorated with small inlaid shell circles. From Susa. 2200 B.C. Archaeology Museum, Tehran. (phot. Museum)*

95 *Grey-black terracotta vase with spout, on a tripod of the same material and colour. From Hasanlu (Azerbaijan). Beginning of the 1st millennium B.C. Archaeology Museum, Tehran. (phot. Museum)*

96 *Rhyton in the shape of an animal's head. Red terracotta with traces of a white coating. The eyes are painted blue. From Ziwiyeh (Kurdistan). 8th–7th century B.C. Archaeology Museum, Tehran. (phot. Museum)*

97 *Bronze object composed of two protomes of animals back-to-back. From Luristan. Beginning of the 1st millennium B.C. Private collection, Geneva. (phot. J. Arlaud)*

98 *Stylized bronze bird. Amulet. From Luristan. Beginning of the 1st millennium B.C. Private collection, Geneva. (phot. J. Arlaud)*

99 *Small humped animal. Bronze. From Gilan. Beginning of the 1st millennium B.C. Private collection, Geneva. (phot. J. Arlaud)*

100 *Vase in the shape of a stylized humped animal (humped bull or zebu). Terracotta. From Gilan. Beginning of the 1st millennium B.C. Archaeology Museum, Tehran. (phot. Museum)*

101 *Terracotta vase with stem, composed of three adjoining bowls connected with each other by two birds and the bust of a person holding a spout. From Hasanlu (Azerbaijan). Beginning of the 1st millennium B.C. Archaeology Museum, Tehran. (phot. Museum)*

102 *Terracotta vase with a quadrangular belly the sides of which are surmounted by a ram's head. From Khurvin. Beginning of the 1st millennium B.C. Archaeology Museum, Tehran. (phot. Museum)*

103 *Cup on three legs. Grey-black terracotta. The belly consists of an animal and two stylized birds. From Hasanlu (Azerbaijan). Beginning of the 1st millennium B.C. Archaeology Museum, Tehran. (phot. Museum)*

104 *Above, a large light-green stone cylinder. Below, a large grey stone cylinder. c. 3000 B.C. Archaeology Museum, Tehran. (phot. Museum)*

105 *Above, a brick-red stone cylinder showing a hunting scene (end of the 2nd millennium B.C.). Below, a black stone cylinder (3rd millennium B.C.) From Luristan. Archaeology Museum, Tehran. (phot. Museum)*

106 *Above, seal of a large agate cylinder showing a hunting scene (c. 1000 B.C.). Below, seal of a large cylinder in brick-red marbled stone (Kassite period, 1500–1000 B.C.) Archaeology Museum, Tehran. (phot. Museum)*

107 *Tablet with proto-Elamitic inscription. About 2900 B.C. Louvre. (phot. Studio Josse)*

108 *Head of prince wearing a notched crown. Lapis-lazuli. From Persepolis. Achaemenid period. 5th century B.C. Archaeology Museum, Tehran. (phot. Museum)*

109 *Watchdog. Black limestone (part of the head has been restored). From Persepolis. Achaemenid period. 6th–5th century B.C. Archaeology Museum, Tehran. (phot. Museum)*

110 *Large pear-shaped bottle. Polished black terracotta. From Hissar III B. c. 2300 B.C. Archaeology Museum, Tehran. (phot. Museum)*

111 *Bronze cup decorated with stylized fleur-de-lis round a central design composed of a garland of fruit (probably pomegranates) joined by festoons. Obtained by Sir Aurel Stein at Luristan. Achaemenid period. c. 6th century B.C. Archaeology Museum, Tehran. (phot. Museum)*

112 *Bronze votive idol. From Luristan. Beginning of the 1st millennium B.C. Archaeology Museum, Tehran. (phot. Museum)*

113 *Idem.*

114 *Vases with spouts, from Necropolis B at Siyalk. 10th–9th century B.C. Left: terracotta copy. Right: specimen in metal. Louvre. (phot. Studio Josse)*

115 *Painted vase from Necropolis B at Siyalk. 10th–9th century B.C. Louvre. (phot. Studio Josse)*

116 *Painted vase with spout from Necropolis B at Siyalk. 10th–9th century B.C. Louvre. (phot. Studio Josse)*

117 *Idem.*

118 *Monochrome bowl decorated with "comb-type" animals. Susa A. Necropolis of Susa. Louvre. (phot. Studio Josse)*

119 *Bowl from Susa. Susa A. Louvre. (phot. Studio Josse)*

120 *Bowl in monochrome terracotta (detail). Susa A. Louvre. (phot. Studio Josse)*

121 *Bowl from Susa with human figure (detail). Susa A. Louvre. (phot. Studio Josse)*

122 *Large solid gold bowl with embossed decoration, engraved with several rows of mythological scenes. In the upper part, gods mounted on chariots. In the lower part, a hero fighting a god of the mountains. From Hasanlu (Azerbaijan). c. 1000 B.C. Archaeology Museum, Tehran. (phot. Museum)*

123 *Large decorated dish from Tepe Djowi. Louvre. (phot. Studio Josse)*

124 *Painted vase from Tepe Giyan. Louvre. (phot. Studio Josse)*

125 *Large goblet from Susa. Susa A. Louvre. (phot. Studio Josse)*

126 *Idem.*

127 *Idem.*

128 *Left: Gold daric. c 400 B.C. Musée d'Art et d'Histoire, Geneva. (phot. J. Arlaud)*
Right: Bodyguards of the King of Kings. Relief in enamelled bricks. Palace of Artaxerxes II (404–359 B.C.) Susa. Louvre. (phot. Museum)

129 *Bowl from Susa A. Necropolis of Susa. Louvre. (phot. Studio Josse)*

130 *Painted vase decorated with panthers and plants. Tepe Siyalk. 4th millennium B.C. Louvre. (phot. Studio Josse)*

131 *Bowl decorated with running greyhounds. Susa A. Necropolis of Susa. Louvre. (phot. Studio Josse)*

132   *Painted potsherd, decorated with an archer. Tepe Djowi. 4th millennium B.C. Louvre. (phot. Studio Josse)*

133   *Painted potsherd, decorated with a frieze of dancers. Rayy. 4th millennium B.C. Louvre. (phot. Studio Josse)*

134   *Painted potsherd, decorated with a bird. Tepe Musyan. Louvre. (phot. Studio Josse)*

135   *Painted monochrome vase, decorated with two birds. Susa II. Louvre. (phot. Studio Josse)*

136   *Monochrome potsherd, decorated with "comb-type" birds. Tepe Giyan V. Louvre. (phot. Studio Josse)*

137   *Small bronze animal with stylized horns. From Gilan. Beginning of the 1st millennium B.C. Archaeology Museum, Tehran. (phot. Museum)*

138   *Gold vase. From Gilan. Beginning of the 1st millennium B.C. Archaeology Museum, Tehran. (phot. Museum)*

139   *Winged ibex (vase-handle). Silver, partly gilded. 4th century B.C. Louvre. (phot. Studio Josse)*

140   *Golden handles in the form of wild goats. Achaemenid. 6th–5th century B.C. Freer Gallery of Art, Washington. (phot. Museum)*

141   *Silver vase with handles in the shape of upright ibexes looking back. From Hamadan. Achaemenid period. 6th–5th century B.C. Archaeology Museum, Tehran. (phot. Museum)*

142   *Large terracotta vase with rounded belly. On the shoulder, stylized birds and sun-shaped designs. From Giyan IV (Mehavend). 2500 B.C. Archaeology Museum, Tehran. (phot. Museum)*

143   *Terracotta vase on stem. The upper part is decorated with a row of ibexes with stylized horns and with geometrical designs painted in black on a cream background. From Siyalk III. 7, c. 3100 B.C. Archaeology Museum, Tehran. (phot. Museum)*

144   *Alabaster statuette of a bear-cub. Susa. Beginning of the 3rd millennium B.C. Louvre. (phot. Studio Josse)*

145   *Protome of roaring lion. Lapis-lazuli. From Persepolis. 5th–4th century B.C. Archaeology Museum, Tehran. (phot. Museum)*

146 *Black stone object with a roaring lion's head sculptured at one end. (Use unknown.) From Persepolis. Achaemenid period. c. 5th century B.C. Archaeology Museum, Tehran. (phot. Museum)*

147 *Gold sword. Pommel decorated with two lion's heads, hilt decorated with ibex's heads. From Hamadan. Achaemenid period. 5th century B.C. Archaeology Museum, Tehran (phot. Museum)*

148 *Whetstone with lion-headed handle. Store of Inshushinak. Middle Elamite. 13th–12th century B.C. Louvre. (phot. Studio Josse)*

149 *Pair of gold bracelets with lion's heads. Susa. Achaemenid era. 4th century B.C. Louvre. (phot. Studio Josse)*

150 *Small gold disc. In the centre, a hero overpowering two lions by holding them by the back paws. Bordered by a circle of triangles surrounded by thin wires. Ziwiyeh (Kurdistan). 8th century B.C. Archaeology Museum, Tehran. (phot. Museum)*

151 *Lapis-lazuli bowl, partly covered with gold leaves. A lion is holding it in its jaws and grasping it with its paws. Beneath, a hand sculptured in bas-relief seems to be carrying it. The belly is decorated with two sphinxes with spreading wings. From Hasanlu (Azerbaijan). c. 850 B.C. Archaeology Museum, Tehran. (phot. Museum)*

152 *Gold rhyton decorated with the* protome *of a winged lion. From Hamadan. Achaemenid period. 5th century B.C. Archaeology Museum, Tehran. (phot. Museum)*

153 *Solid gold sword. The inlay of the handle has disappeared. From: Kalardasht (Mazanderan). 9th century B.C. Archaeology Museum, Tehran. (phot. Museum)*

Printed in Switzerland

THE TEXT AND ILLUSTRATIONS
IN THIS VOLUME WERE PRINTED
ON THE PRESSES OF NAGEL
PUBLISHERS IN GENEVA.

FINISHED IN AUGUST 1965.
BINDING BY NAGEL PUBLISHERS,
GENEVA.

PLATES ENGRAVED BY AMOR S.A.
GENEVA

LEGAL DEPOSIT NR. 368

PRINTED IN SWITZERLAND